A Resilient Life

A Cop's Journey in Pursuit of Purpose

By

David Berez

Cover design by: Mark Thoburn, Thoburn Design & Illustrations
Edited by Natalie June Reilly

While the stories in this book are all true and accurate to the best of my own recollection, the names and identities of those associated with the stories have been changed to protect the privacy of the individual. Additionally, some geographical locations have also been altered for the same reason.

Advance Praise for
A Resilient Life: A Cop's Journey in Pursuit of Purpose

"The war on our cops by politicians and the press has had significant consequences for public safety and for the well-being of those brave enough to protect our communities. Through his intensely personal story, David Berez captures the emotional toll that wearing the badge can have on our nation's cops. His powerful story of service, struggle and survival is a must read for those wishing to genuinely understand what our police really face on the beat, the impact of politics on policing, the crisis of police suicide, and the national challenge of protecting those who protect us. *A Resilient Life* also brings a sense of hope to all those dealing with pain that clouds their future. Berez's story is one we need now more than ever because it proves that light can triumph over darkness."

—Tom Basile, Newsmax TV Anchor,
Washington Times Columnist and Author

"David is a gifted writer whose own life journey has guided him to create a book that is both powerful and timely. The law enforcement community has been battered for years, not just physically but emotionally. It is the nature of policing. David has put into words the thoughts and feelings of many who serve behind the badge, and this book will touch all who read it."

—Lt. Randy Sutton (Ret) Las Vegas Metro Police
and Founder of The Wounded Blue

"The average person will experience three or four traumatic events in their lifetime. The average police officer will experience 400–600 traumatic events. Nevertheless, we expect our law enforcement professionals to be perfect and indestructible. David Berez, a 20-year police veteran, opens his soul in this riveting book, 'A Resilient Life,' to remind us that cops are human, and while policing is honorable and purposeful, there is a hefty price to pay. Confronted with the suicides of two police officers he was very close to, a parental and police leadership structure that failed him, and battling suicidal thoughts of his own, David found a way to survive—and to thrive—as a husband, parent, police officer and friend. For those of us who have never worn the badge, David lets us know what the journey is like—the good, the bad and the ugly. Having read his story, we owe David and all who serve and protect a heartfelt 'Thank You.'"

—*Craig W. Floyd, President and CEO of Citizens Behind the Badge*
and Founding CEO (Emeritus) of the
National Law Enforcement Officers Memorial Fund

any more police officers, and I live every day to keep my word. Your life and your death will not have been in vain.

... to my Mom; if you were here, I think you would be proud. You would have struggled to believe that I wrote a book, but you would be proud of me—the police officer, the husband, the dad, and the man I became. Your Bunz Bear is all grown up.

Table of Contents

Reflections: Crystal Ball

INTRODUCTION

"If I am not for myself, who will be for me?
If I am only for myself, what am I?
And if not now, when?"
–Rabbi Hillel

I have spent more than 30 years proudly serving my community in different capacities, and I stood tall through it all. I collected 100 lifetimes' worth of experiences and believed each would make me stronger for the next. What I failed to realize and what shaped the second half of my life was that all that learned and lived experience was never properly processed and, therefore, not actually making me stronger. The fundamental detail, the part of the job that nobody in law enforcement talks about, had an even greater impact on me.

*The challenge was what I **did not** know.*

I did not know that the memories of these experiences would be stored away in a box that would eventually reopen, or should I say, explode open? I did not know that each incident was a building block to an eventual post-traumatic response. I did not understand that I would live with these events for the rest of my life.

The head-on car crash on an icy road, killing two of the three children onboard and emotionally destroying the father behind the wheel. To my dying day, I will hear the shrills of despair from this man. The death notification of a 17-year-old boy to his parents following his suicide on the train tracks. Seeing the emptiness in his mother's eyes and hearing the squeal of her voice as I explained to her why she could not see her son's body one last time or give him one last hug.

I will never forget holding a 10-year-old child in my arms as my partners (unsuccessfully) performed CPR on the only parent he had and then being the one to tell this child that he was now an orphan. To this day, I relive reviving a childhood friend following an overdose in the bathroom of a bar, the needle still dangling from his arm. I see the mangled body of another childhood friend with a Broadway career in her future, still stuck behind the steering wheel after she was broadsided by an 18-wheeler.

I can still *see* the battered women, the abused children, the suicide hanging from the tree, the day laborer who fell into the commercial woodchipper on a rainy day. I *hear* the screams of a heartbroken parent, the screeching tires of my own car crashes, *the* loudest gun blast followed by deafening silence. I *smell* burning flesh, a rotting corpse, accelerants from arson fires, the ashes of a struggling man's business, the odor of alcohol on the breath of a soccer mom sitting behind the wheel of her minivan with heavy front-end damage, having just killed someone else's child. I can still *taste* the dust from the two fallen towers.

But the fifth sense, *touch*, is the one I am challenged by the most. While my body aches from years of carrying the physical and emotional weight of the job and other life experiences, it is the lack of touch where I endure the most pain. I can no longer feel my mother's embrace. I struggle to hug my own kids, and I am challenged by the inability to show affection to my wife because through it all, I have lost the ability to feel love.

If you aren't in law enforcement, and even if you are, you are probably asking yourself, "Why would anyone in their right mind want to become a cop?" For me, like many of my brothers and sisters, it was my passion to help others. That passion began in 1989 at the age of 14 years old. I wanted to grow up to be a doctor, so I joined the volunteer rescue squad and began what I believed would be a long career in medicine. By 16 years old, I earned my EMT certification, along with many other secondary rescue certificates. By the age of 18, I was certified as a heavy rescue technician, pre-hospital trauma life support provider, and several other specialties.

I was well on my way to achieving my goals.

From a tender age, not quite fully developed into adulthood, I was exposed to horrific car crashes, burn victims, drownings, gunshot wounds, suicides, homicides, and infants whose lives I could not save. As my EMS experience mounted, along with my overall exposure to emergency services, I retooled my professional goals and decided to become a police officer. To me, it was a noble career. I would be able to help others, serve and engage my community, receive specialized training and be a part of a revered fraternity. Not to mention, the pay for a police officer in New Jersey was about three times that of an EMT.

In college, I tested the waters of law enforcement while working for the university's public safety department. I participated in two internships and earned a dual degree in sociology and criminal justice. The first of the two internships was with the Freeport Police Department (New York). It was there that I was introduced to the worst of humanity when I helped to investigate the murder of an infant child who died at the hands of a parent. The second internship was with the East Windsor Police Department (New Jersey), where I ended up spending my career.

During my college years, I continued to volunteer as an EMT back home in East Windsor and on Long Island with the Uniondale Fire Department. I was exposed to many different calls for service and rescue missions, up to and including a passenger plane crash. It was also during my college tenure that I was faced with suicide for the first time. One of my mentors, a detective sergeant who worked in East Windsor, took his own life. He would become the subject of my senior thesis on Critical Incident Stress Management (CISM).

After graduating college, I had the good fortune of spending one year as a medico/legal intern with the New York City Medical Examiner's Office. I assisted with any and all death investigations (on scene and autopsy) that occurred in Manhattan. It was anything from unattended elderly deaths to mob hits, from drownings (floaters) to rooftop jumpers and arson victims (crispy critters) and beyond. I have literally seen and smelled it all. And after all these years, I can still see and smell many of those cases.

I graduated from the police academy in 1999, beginning my professional career as a police officer. Many interesting experiences occurred early on that gave shape to the path my career would take, but none more impactful than September 11, 2001. I was off-duty that day, but upon hearing the news, I jumped out of bed and headed into work where I met my partner.

Gear bags ready for deployment, ready to save the world.

Our agency, however, made it clear that they were not sending anyone into the City because, and I quote, "Not our town; not our problem."

With a bewildered look on our faces, my partner and I hopped into my personal car and drove up to Jersey City. From there, we boarded a fire boat that took us into lower Manhattan. We engaged in any way we could, serving to the best of our ability. While much of my time spent at Ground Zero remains as fuzzy as the photos I took that day, the sights, smells, sounds and feelings are crystal clear. The experience shaped who I would become as both a police officer and as a man.

I learned perspective.

I learned priorities.

I learned friendship and brotherhood.

What I did not know was how long I would live with the nightmares. Still, my career marched on, and I continued to play a variety of roles in my community. I had many experiences and was fortunate to network with a lot of people. The good times and the positive impact I made are too many to count and recall, but I was a part of it, and it gives me great joy and pride in knowing that.

It was truly an honor.

However, the moments of tragedy and loss have impacted me the most. Fast forward to December 2019; I was still haunted by a look of sadness and despair, but only when I looked in the mirror. I still smelled the odor of alcohol, but it was on my own breath. I still heard a parent's desperate cry, but it stopped when I woke up from the nightmares.

As I battle through 30 years' worth of memories, I find peace when I see the light in my children's eyes and the comfort in their hearts when I wake them up every morning and tuck them into bed every night. I sense my wife's relief, no longer worrying when or if I am coming home. I recognize my own strength, both physical and mental, when I return from a 50-mile bike ride, successfully working through a new challenge or achieving a new goal.

I recently lost a good friend of mine and a member of my Blue Family to suicide. I realize, not only am I not alone in my emotions, but I am in a much better place than many. My friend struggled with betrayal on many levels, from work to home to the betrayal of his own mental health. Following his death, I experienced a feeling of guilt, like I had never experienced before.

As I worked to resolve my own guilt and pain, once again, I found purpose in helping others. I started by writing an article that reached over 15,000 people before it was even published nationwide. I then connected with another retired colleague who was the chief resilience officer for the county where I worked and lived. The resiliency program was what I needed for my own health and to help others because, *"if not now, when?"*

In September 2020, I enrolled in the Resiliency Program Officer (RPO) course hosted by the Mercer County Prosecutor's Office. This program is based on growing your Pre-boom Toolkit and the concept of a growth mindset following a post-traumatic response. Post-traumatic responses can be the result of a single incident or a lifetime of experiences. In either case, a resilient mind must be formed to grow a stronger sense of self and a life worth living.

Resiliency comes from four basic domains: mental, physical, social, and spiritual. Each domain then has several tenets. As noted in the New Jersey Resiliency Program instructor manual, *"Mental health is the ability to effectively cope with the unique mental stressors and challenges. Physical health is the ability to adopt and sustain healthy behaviors needed to enhance health and wellbeing. Social health is the ability to engage in healthy social networks that promote overall wellbeing and optimal performance. Spiritual health is the ability to strengthen a set of beliefs, principles or values that sustain an individual's sense of wellbeing and purpose."*

The Resiliency Program opened my mind to "counting my blessings," "accomplishing goals," "checking my playbook," "balancing my thinking," "capitalizing my strengths," and "acceptance strategies for mindfulness." As I apply these lessons and include physical and spiritual resilience, I strive to live more, love stronger, play harder and find inner peace. While I work daily on becoming a better me, I find the sweet spot in life is to help others find their "best self," too.

It is the "balance" that Rabbi Hillel refers to. This balance has helped me to see more smiles in my mirror, lean on fewer crutches to ease the pain, and enjoy a quieter mind for a more peaceful sleep. While I may never master the art, myself, I will forever be a student of the craft and share my own journey with others so that they, too, can learn from my wins and learned lessons. Together, as we embrace these challenging times, I hope you will join me in the conversation regarding resiliency and policing.

As we move from one chapter of life to the next, resiliency is how we turn the page. We must take what we have learned and apply it to where we are in the present, the here and now, so that when tomorrow comes, we are equipped to do our best. If you are lost and struggling, find someone who can help light your path. If your path is well lit, find someone with whom you can share your light. Remember, in our Blue Family, no one fights alone. Stay resilient and live a life full of purpose.

*This world is better because **you** are in it.*

CHAPTER ONE
You are ACEs

The Center for Disease Control (CDC) defines Adverse Childhood Experiences (ACEs) as "potentially traumatic events that occur in childhood. ACEs can include violence, abuse, and growing up in a family with mental health or substance use problems. Toxic stress from ACEs can change brain development and affect how the body responds to stress."

While I did not grow up in a physically violent household, my parents had a tumultuous relationship. Verbal abuse and fighting were a regular thing. My father was an absent parent who was more concerned about screwing his secretary than he was being home to screw in a lightbulb or teach me how to use a screwdriver.

He was everything I knew I did not want to be.

He lied on our taxes if he actually filed them at all. He cheated on my mother and was a complete failure as a father. Some of my parents' fights were even cause for a police response. I remember those officers well and the shared disdain they had for my father for being a total douche.

My mother, on the other hand, was a kind soul who worked hard to feed our family and raise me and my sister with good core values rooted in our family's Jewish traditions. We went to the synagogue almost every Friday night for services, and the Temple families were our community. My biggest gripe was that The Dukes of Hazzard aired on Friday nights at eight o'clock which, regrettably, conflicted with Shabbat services. This was long before we owned a VCR. For those born after 1990, a VCR is like a DVR, only not as sleek and sexy. It was a large machine with a video tape the size of a box of cigars and a record button. If you came from a bougie family, yours may have also had a rewind button.

Truth is, everything about The Dukes of Hazzard conflicted with being Jewish in the suburbs. I always loved it though. Somehow, it connected me to my redneck roots that I never had. To this day, I am just a "good ol' boy, ain't never meanin' no harm." I also rock Tecovas boots, a big-ass belt buckle, plaid shirts, and a barn jacket. I listen to country music. I love NASCAR, and I drink 'shine from a mason jar, usually in the solace surrounding a fire pit. And while my heart resides in a place that looks a lot like Hazzard County or East Tennessee, my feet are firmly planted in New Jersey, at least for now.

While the "ACEs" in my family most certainly had an effect on my life, there were a few wildcards outside the home that played a hand in how I turned out. For example, when I was seven years old, I had a T & A, following a lifelong history of strep throat and sinus infections. For those with a woke or warped mind, getting a T & A in 1982 had nothing to do with gender reassignment. It was the removal of my tonsils and adenoids.

Glad we got that straightened out.

I spent seven years fighting infections and then seven days in the hospital with some of the coolest people in my life at that time—doctors. They seemed to be able to fix just about anything that was hurting. That was the first time I identified with the concept of purpose, and I decided I wanted to become a doctor, particularly a pediatrician, so I could help sick kids like me feel better.

Another wild card that had an impact on my life, something I never really talked about, was a guy named Herb. He and his wife, Louise, were longtime friends of my maternal grandparents and lived only a few towns over from us. Louise resembled Jabba the Hutt and spent most of her time sitting in a chair, occasionally slithering from one place to another. Herb was a physically healthy person and an amateur photographer. He especially loved taking pictures of kids. My mom and grandmother would always take him up on the offer to take pictures of my sister and me.

Their philosophy was "Free is for me!"

What they did not know was that I was the one paying the price, a hefty price. My sister always went first, followed by a few obligatory group shots and then he would shoot me. He would tell my family to take a walk because he liked the privacy of being alone with me. He presented as a creep with his lanky fingers and wiry unkempt hair. I would learn over time that he *was* a creep. There is no telling how many times Herb touched me in various places that would be considered criminal sexual contact, making odd comments as if what he was doing was normal and something I should enjoy. All I know is that it happened before I was old enough to realize it was wrong or even understand what the fuck was going on.

I don't remember when it started, but I do remember the last time he tried touching me. I was about nine years old. We were on a playground in a park in Franklin Township, New Jersey. He had me put on a bright shirt and a pair of shorts that he brought to the "photo shoot." He liked seeing me in oversized men's clothes, and these were his clothes. This was his perverted fantasy. I was reluctant to change, but my mom told me to put on the clothes. She said, "The pictures will be great. You'll look so cute."

I looked like a flamenco dancer in Miami in the early 80s. I was standing on the jungle gym, and Herb was positioning me in suggestive, flamboyant poses. I watched as the rest of my family walked away. I was scared and disgusted. I knew what was coming and did not want him

3

touching me. I stood silent for a few pictures before running away. I chased after my mom, crying and trying to explain what had been happening.

No one believed me.

"You are imagining things," my mom said. "No one would ever do such a repulsive thing, especially not Herb and especially not to you."

Herb was quick to call it quits on the photo shoot, and we all went our separate ways. As much as my family denied my claims, refusing to validate what I had been telling them, we never did see Herb and Louise again. To be honest, the next time I heard about them was when they died.

Good riddance!

Throughout my childhood trials and tribulations, the "ACE" in the hole was when I turned 14 years old. I joined the local volunteer rescue squad. I had done so for a few reasons. Firstly, as I mentioned, I wanted to be a doctor. Knowing that I was no Doogie Howser, MD (another social reference that dates my youth), and there was no chance I was going to graduate high school, college, and medical school that year, I decided to volunteer. You see, I loved school so much that I actually took Algebra-I twice, and at that rate, high school seemed more like a lifelong career rather than a four-year experience to jumpstart my formal education.

Secondly, I joined the squad to escape my house, a place I always wanted to come back to, but never wanted to be around. My father was gone by then. He left when I turned 13, just after my bar mitzvah. The photographs from that event are actually the last I have of him, the obligatory family shot on the altar in front of the Torah.

My house was full of mixed emotions, comforting like a mother's embrace, yet consumed with the sound of angry yelling, even when there was an empty silence. I recall the music of John Denver and The Beatles, mixed with Peter, Paul and Mary and Simon and Garfunkel. I remember the sound of my mother crying when she thought she was alone, reminiscing of when love filled our home. I can still smell holiday dinners and the stench of cigarettes when my father lit up in the garage. Looking back, I told myself I joined the rescue squad to save others, but really ... I was hoping to save myself.

This would be a theme throughout my life.

From a very young age, I excelled in the field of emergency services. I became a hardened soul fairly quickly. By the time I was 16 years old, I was a certified EMT and was responding to all calls for service. My pager would alert me with emergency tones, and the adrenaline rush would send me into superman mode.

I changed into my jumpsuit like Clark Kent in a phone booth, grabbing my web belt with all my cool rescue tools. I slung my stethoscope around my neck, like a true medical professional, and I ran out of the house, to the end of my driveway. I waited there, hoping an older volunteer, one with a driver's license, would drive past my house with their blue lights flashing. If they were paying attention, they would see me on the sidewalk, waving my arms. I was so amped up, I was prepared to get a running start, so they would not even have to stop to let me in.

I enjoyed it when my friend, Seth, would pick me up. He was my sister's age and drove a real piece of shit Plymouth, a red, two-door. Picture DeeDee McCall's car from the 80s police series *Hunter*. The passenger door was just for looks, as it was wedged closed and rendered useless. I would have to jump through the window while the car was practically still moving. That made it all the more exciting.

Bo and Luke Duke would have been proud!

Imagine how much sooner I could have mastered the art of jumping through car windows had I gone to synagogue a little less and watched The Dukes of Hazzard a little more!

I saw everything, from traumatic car crashes to domestic abuse victims, from unsuccessfully reviving newborns who had suffered from sudden infant death syndrome to decomposed bodies found by a neighbor after noticing a buildup of flies on the windows of the house across the street. I was exposed to far too many of life's most horrific events, far too often. We never debriefed, and we never talked about what we saw, what we did, or how any given incident affected us.

We were badass volunteers, known locally as the "Jolly Vollies."

The human brain, as we know, is not fully formed until somewhere around the age of 21. That said, I had been taking in all of these Adverse Childhood Experiences, storing them away without processing them. My experiences may somewhat differ from the reason the ACE's concept was originally studied, but that did not change the fact that my developing brain took on a lot at a young and formative age. Moreover, I did not know how to properly deal with any of it. So, I didn't.

My ACEs score is 5 out of 10. This puts me at high risk for toxic stress. Toxic stress includes self-destructive behaviors, such as depression, anxiety, ADHD, aggression, alcohol abuse, and self-harm. The average person (67-percent of the American population) has a score of 1. Only 13-percent of Americans have a score equal to or higher than 5. What does this mean?

It means if you aren't seeking support, you are fucked!

My volunteer EMS career continued through college and at home in East Windsor. I even rose to the ranks of captain and deputy chief. While attending Hofstra University in Long Island, I also rode for the Uniondale Fire Department in New York.

While I continue to hold a "Life Member" status with the East

Windsor Township Rescue Squad—District 1, my time in EMS came to an end at the age 24 when I took a full-time job as a police officer in East Windsor, the town where I grew up.

Transgenerational Trauma—The Prequel to ACEs

Transgenerational trauma is not trauma that self-identifies as someone else. This is your trauma; you own it, and it was gifted to you by your parents, grandparents and the overall history of your family's journey. The trauma response from transgenerational factors can manifest in a variety of ways—biologically, socially, mentally, and/or emotionally.

For example, if you are a woman whose family genealogy is rooted as Ashkenazi Jews, you are 10 times more likely to have the BRCA2 gene which causes breast cancer. This is certainly a traumatic precursor that can shape your story.

If your family fell victim to mass genocide, like mine did, this likely shaped how you were raised, effecting you mentally, socially, and emotionally. Families with a history of financial struggles, sexual abuse, and poor education are most likely to perpetuate transgenerational trauma. However, that cycle can be broken, and the transition can start with you.

We carry the heavy baggage of the family that came before us, but if we learn from the contents inside the baggage and then leave it behind, we can change the trajectory of our future. Not only that, but we shed the unnecessary weight and that high ACEs score ends with you.

What I know of my family history goes back less than 100 years, but that history had a great influence on my childhood and beyond. For the first half of my life, I certainly carried the bags of my ancestors, but over time I learned to only take the good from those bags and use the experiences that served me best. I ditched the heaviest weight that was holding me back.

I will go deeper into my family history in a later chapter, but the challenges that my ancestors endured, mostly for being Jewish, impacted the way my parents were raised, and in turn, the way they raised me. It shaped my values, priorities, and goals. However, it positively influenced my understanding of *"What's Important Now,"* allowing me to forge a path forward, always making decisions that are best for my family.

I have always prioritized my family and friends, often at the expense of my own self-care—physically and mentally. I know now I must take care of myself in order to take care of others. However, it must be a conscious effort, and this does not come naturally to me. Just as the safety instructions on a commercial airline instruct, one must always first put on their own oxygen mask before they help someone else.

Transgenerational trauma is real, and while you do not have a choice whether or not to carry the bags that were passed down to you from your ancestors, you do have a choice on how to deal with the stuff inside. By learning from and dealing with what is inside those bags, you can lighten the load for yourself and the next generation, making the bags easier to carry.

CHAPTER TWO
Bag 'Em & Tag 'Em

After graduating high school by the skin of my teeth, I was accepted into Hofstra University through a special program called New College. It was a "last chance" at a formal education for high school failures who had potential. Truth be told, that was the first time anyone in my life acknowledged that I had "potential," so I jumped at the chance. After completing the college initiation courses, specifically a course called Research Methods (learning to read, write, and comprehend beyond a third-grade level), I was allowed to begin my freshman year. Those courses were designed to give guys like me a fighting chance at earning a diploma.

I needed all the help I could get.

That first semester, I was forced to take botany. I wanted to be a doctor ... remember? Yeah, that didn't go well. I failed my first college course. I failed because it was hard, and I quit. My entire life I wanted to be a doctor, and I could not even pass one simple course on plant cells. I felt like such a failure, and I all but gave up on my education. It was the first time I felt like I lost my identity when I realized becoming a doctor was not in my future.

When I went home for winter break, I met up with a police officer in my hometown. His name was Todd. He and I became friends while I was a volunteer on the rescue squad. Todd was like a cool, older brother.

I really looked up to him.

It was 0100 hours on Christmas Eve. Todd was working the

holiday shift. I was on call for the squad, driving an old police car turned EMS first responder vehicle. I remember meeting up with Todd in a dark parking lot behind a pharmaceutical company known as LavaPharm. We were catching up on life. He was telling me cop stories, and I am not sure I realized it at that time, but that conversation changed my life forever.

A couple weeks later, I showed up to school a few days early so that I could meet with the registrar and reshuffle the deck for what would be my reimagined college experience. I changed my major from pre-med to pre-cop. I became a sociology and criminal justice double major. When my mom got the tuition bill for the second semester, along with the new course schedule, she was puzzled. She asked, "Was there a mix up with your course selection? Why are there a bunch of criminal justice classes on your schedule?"

"Nope! No mix up," I replied. "I'm gonna be a cop!"

It was the first time I said it out loud.

I had found my new identity.

I can still hear her voice when she said, "You are going to do WHAT?" With each class and internship experience, I knew that law enforcement was exactly where I needed to be. I was going to help people, which is why I wanted to be a doctor in the first place. Same purpose; different mission. Going into law enforcement, I was going to be in a position to make kids' lives better, not with my hands but with my heart.

I knew I had this.

It took some convincing, but my mom continued to pay the tuition bill, and eventually she came to terms with my decision. She said, "I truly do not care what you do for a living, just be the best one doing it." I am not sure that I believed her, and I am not sure she believed in me, but it was exactly what I needed to hear.

I was well into my college career when I came home for Thanksgiving in the fall of 1996. The first stop I made when I got into town was the rescue squad. There were a bunch of cars in the parking lot, including some police cars and a few EMS vehicles from the county and neighboring jurisdictions.

It was odd.

I knew something wasn't right. It was that same feeling you get when the phone rings at an odd hour of the night and caller ID reads: "Someone died."

When I walked into the building, the mood was somber and silent. "Who died?" I asked, jokingly.

Everyone looked at me like I was an insensitive prick. Vivian shouted, "No one called you?"

"About what?" I replied, sounding confused.

"Johnny O. committed suicide this morning in the front lot of the police station," Vivian sighed.

Detective Sergeant John O'Donnell was one of my idols. He was a squared-away dude who was a rising star in the police department and was well on his way to becoming chief. He was one of the officers who had often responded to my house when my parents were fighting. Hearing the news, I felt like I had lost a piece of myself.

He was ACEs!

It took me a long time to process Johnny O.'s death. To be honest, I am not sure I ever really did. To this day, the truth behind his suicide has never been openly discussed. His death was my first step into learning about the mental health crisis of first responders.

I topped off my on-campus education with a senior thesis on the topic of Critical Incident Stress Management (CISM), following a summer internship with the East Windsor Police. My paper was dedicated in honor and in memory of Johnny O. May he rest in eternal peace.

"Johnny, I hope the demons you were fighting were unable to follow you to Valhalla."

My college career came to an end, and I, to the surprise of many, graduated with a bachelor's degree. Like most college grads, I needed to figure out what was next. My buddy and fraternity brother, Chris, knew it was my goal to become a police officer. He told me that his Aunt Theresa worked as an investigator for the New York City Medical Examiner and was married to a detective in the NYPD. Chris was to connect me and the detective, so that I could learn from him and understand what it would take to get into the police academy. I was so excited, but I did not hear anything past the words, "My Aunt Theresa is an investigator for the New York City Medical Examiner's Office ..." I seriously thought I could be part doctor and part cop.

Holy shit! That would be my dream job!

I met Aunt Theresa, and she hooked me up with an internship at the Office of the Chief Medical Examiner in Manhattan. I spent an entire year learning about dead people, conducting scene investigations, and assisting (observing) autopsies. I had seven lifetimes of education in a matter of months. I was introduced to them all, from floaters to crispy critters, from jumpers (off buildings) to mashers (suicide by train), and from mob hits to decomps.

If you can die from it, I have seen it!

Every morning, we would have a list of cases that occurred overnight. We would grab a bagel and tea for breakfast, hop into the 1988

Chevy Blazer, and traverse the City with lights and sirens as if the deceased were getting impatient because of how long it took us to get there. Once on scene, we gave the body a once-over, taking pictures and notes. Then we would "bag 'em and tag 'em." The remains would get stuffed into a leak-proof bag and the orderlies would toss the body into the refrigerated storage van, and then we would all race to the next scene.

I was assigned to an investigator, someone I really hit it off with. His name was Shyia, and he happened to be an Orthodox Jew. Shyia was a full-time investigator with OCME but moonlighted as a cantor at a local synagogue in Brooklyn. While I was not religious like he was, we bonded on account of the fact we were both Jewish, and we had a mutual love for music, although our tastes were quite different. He was not much into Metallica, Soundgarden, and Nirvana, which were my favorites at the time.

I was not yet a real country fan.

Shyia would often meet me halfway with Billy Joel and The Beatles. I remember introducing him to the songs of my musical crush, Leann Rimes, who, looking back, was my introduction to country music. All he could say about her music was that she was "very breathy."

Ugh, what a letdown.

Anyway, when the bodies were brought back to the morgue, they were placed onto aluminum tables in the climate-controlled examination room. There were seven stations. Autopsies were conducted in the morning by the forensic pathologists, and I had an open invitation to "observe." I will never forget my first experience watching a human body be cut open and dissected. It was a far cry from 9th grade biology when we dissected frogs and owl pellets.

The doctor grabbed the scalpel and made the first incision from the right shoulder to the top of the sternum and then again from the left shoulder. The third incision was made, starting from the point where the first two incisions met, down to and around the navel, landing just before the pubic line. Next, the doctor separated the skin from the muscle and fileted the body like a freshly caught tuna. The organs were removed one by one, each being examined and weighed. All the major blood vessels were hand traced, looking for ruptures, clogs and disease.

For me, the wildest and most memorable part of the autopsy was the head. The doctor would start by cutting the scalp from ear to ear, across the top of the head, pulling the skin forward and peeling the face off to expose the skull. The same would be done for the back half of the scalp. An electric reciprocating saw was used to cut through the bone of the skull, particles of white dust blowing about and the smell of burning bone rising from the heat of the saw blade. The brain was removed with precision and examined quite carefully before being weighed. Once the head was closed and the face pressed back on, the final step was to stick a large gauge needle into the eyeballs and remove the vitreous fluid. The fluid was saved for testing, and saline was used to refill the eye.

Samples of tissue from each organ were removed and sent to the lab, but for the most part, everything else was bagged and placed back into the body cavity before being sewn up with wire, resembling the likes of Frankenstein. To this day, I still see, smell, hear, and feel every single part of my first autopsy—an overweight man with multiple gunshot wounds. I was only a few observations into my OCME experience when I was given a scalpel and invited to make the cuts myself. It was an out of body experience that made me feel disconnected from the human body. I have never been able to look at people the same again. When I look at you, I have a bit of x-ray vision, and I wonder what you have going on beneath the flesh.

Creepy, I know.

My favorite cases were those individuals who died from a gunshot wound, much like my first autopsy experience. Prior to the first cut, we would check for holes, and we would label them as entry or exit wounds. We would then insert long probes intended to trace the path of the bullet. Then, when we cut open the body, we could determine which bullet caused what damage. The forensics of homicide cases continued to interest me for the duration of my career. As a police officer, I had the opportunity to investigate three cases, and my experience at the medical examiner's office proved to be invaluable. Time in the morgue was an education I could not have acquired anywhere else in life. Yes, my exposure to death taught me a lot about life—an odd pun for sure! But my exposure to so much trauma was something I never really considered and certainly never addressed.

I would not trade my experience at OCME for anything. It was the best education I ever had. I most certainly think about many of those cases when I close my eyes at night, especially the case that literally hit home when I unknowingly married into it just a few years later. It's not my story to tell, so I won't.

CHAPTER THREE
Jersey Shore

As my internship with the Office of the Chief Medical Examiner was nearing an end, I connected with one of East Windsor Police Department's rising stars, Harry, who (years later) became the chief of police. From early childhood, I formed great relationships with the officers of this department. I am thankful they always treated me like a little brother all those years. Harry, being the guy he is, leveraged his professional network and supported my application to the Seaside Park Police Department, where he, too, started his career.

In New Jersey, there are a few ways to break into law enforcement. For starters, we have two types of affiliated agencies—civil service and chief's test. For all civil service affiliated agencies, a candidate takes a common, state-issued, written test and is ranked based on score. Candidates are eligible for the town and county agencies in which they live. Those agencies then choose from the top-scoring test takers, inviting these candidates for an interview. Depending upon how the interview goes, a background check will follow and if the candidate's background checks out, an offer is made.

For those applying to an agency based on the New Jersey Chief of Police Standards, a candidate may have to test for the individual agency or, more likely than not, apply with a resume, sit for an interview and then wait for a background check. This process is much more subjective, catering to candidates who are already certified and/or know someone in that particular agency. Then there is the New Jersey Boardwalk Warriors.

That is how I got my start.

Harry introduced me to the Seaside Park Police chief with a wink and a nod, and I was able to take it from there. I was hired as a Class I Special Police Officer for the summer of 1998. As a Class I, I received basic training on arrest, search and seizure, PR-24 side-handled baton, handcuffing, and ticket writing for parking and local ordinance violations. As a Class I, I was on bike patrol, drove the Cushman cart, and walked the boardwalk. On occasion, I rode the ATV on the beach and the jet ski in the bay. As the summer months began to wind down, I worked as needed through fall. I had little to no training, was full of wanna-be-cop energy and had no fucking idea what I was doing.

It was the best job ever!

On January 2, 1999, I entered the Ocean County Police Academy. This was the best 19.5 weeks I would ***never*** want to do again. I was never a real muscular or strong guy, but I could run as if the devil, himself, was chasing me. And quite frankly, I think that's why I am still here to this day.

More on that later.

From PT (physical training) at the beach, to low crawls through the goose shit, to pushups until my arms gave out, to falling face first into the goose shit, I hated it so much, but I loved who I was becoming. One of the most humbling experiences was Boxing Day. No ... not the holiday celebrated across the pond the day after Christmas, but rather the day when recruits were paired up with a partner and went to the mat.

We beat the shit out of each other.

It was the first time I was ever punched in the face (Thanks, Bucci!), but it was a lesson I needed and one that would prove its worth early in my career. I was never going to quit as a recruit, and my instructors were building me up into the best version of myself. Both my body and mind were being broken down and rebuilt from the ground up.

I got good at telling myself to suck it up.

In the words of the storied Marine, Chesty Puller, "Pain is just weakness leaving the body." I graduated with shin splints, a broken toe, a warped sense of reality, and a sheepdog's mindset. That is to say, there are wolves and there are sheep, and I was put on this earth to stand in between the two. I was put here to protect the flock from the evil that exists in the world.

This *is my purpose!*

The police academy is like any other paramilitary basic training program. It takes an average individual, breaks them down—mentally and physically—then builds them back up again, only stronger and with the knowledge of how to be the most effective at the job. It is a one-size fits all program, and it is up to you to decide what you will get out of it. It all depends on how hard you push yourself.

This training philosophy has evolved over the years. At the end of 2022, following three years of community, political, and special interest calls for change in policing strategies, the Police Executive Research Forum, a widely recognized think tank, has issued a paper titled, *Transforming Police Recruit Training: 40 Guiding Principles.* I am positive this will be the national guideline for 21st Century police training.

I have mixed feelings about the change. I love the old-school way of training, as caveman as it sounds, because it filters out the weak of mind and body. It has a Darwinian modality; only the strongest among us will survive. It pushes individuals beyond their comfort zone for those who are willing to take that chance, allowing for growth beyond one's perceived potential.

In other words, you realize your actual capabilities.

The police academy, if you give it all you've got, will take you in, chew you up and spit out the best version of who you are. However, through this process, we are often stripped of raw emotion, compassion, and empathy. We are hardened for the purpose of survival and sharpened to a point that is often not relatable to the purpose of our service. It is difficult to train as both a lion and a lamb, but if we can train more like the shepherd, a true servant leader, I believe we can be more effective in the communities we serve.

I graduated with my academy brothers (no sisters) in Class #72 of the Ocean County Police Academy. Honestly, it was one of *the* proudest days of my life. For so many years, people told me that my goals were too lofty, and I would probably never turn out to be much of anything. They all doubted me. From teachers to family to my own mother, this moment was the biggest "fuck you!"

I made the decision to embark on this journey on my own. I built the network, so that I could get my foot in the door. I passed all the tests to enter the academy. I fought like hell, despite a broken body and developing mind to get to this moment.

I did this!

And for the first time in my life, I was proud of myself. I loved the new me. My mom, both my grandmothers, my sister, and my best friends were present at my graduation from the police academy in May of 1999. They were all proud of my accomplishment, but my relationship with my mom would never be the same. She resented it, not only that I became a cop, but that I had become something.

Something other than nothing.

The same "nothing" she expected of me. To this day, I think she hated the fact that I did this without her, and that I was not a failure. As her youngest child, I was now a grown-ass man who she could no longer control. No matter how hard she pushed my sister to succeed, and my sister is a complete rock star, I think my mom wanted me to grow up to be a loser.

Why do I say this?

She regularly told me I was a loser. I am convinced she did this so that I would live in her basement forever, and it would give her something to complain about and someone to be superior to. My mom and maternal grandmother hated men. My grandmother just thought men were useful idiots, but my mom harbored true hatred and resentment. She wanted the men in her life to fail. I think it all goes back to how my father failed her, their marriage, and our family.

After the academy, I immediately returned to the Seaside Park Police Department to serve as a Class II Special Police Officer. On duty, this part-time position gave me full authority of law enforcement in the state of New Jersey, but when I punched out at the end of shift, I was just Dave Berez. This was probably the best summer of my life. I was 23 years old, the same year Blink 182 came out with the song "What's my age again?"

I had the world by the balls.

Everything about me, from the uniform to the fresh-out-of-the-academy body and attitude, to the level of self-confidence that would make Trump blush, had the highest CDI (*Chicks Dig It*) factor you could imagine. I was patrolling one of the nation's most notorious shore towns.

Thanks, MTV!

I had a badge, a gun and my lifelong best friend, Adam, who was a Class I Special Police Officer. Adam's Dad, who was a police officer in the town I grew up, has always been like a father to me. To this day, he was one of the few people in my life who pushed me (and Adam) to be our best. He did so because he wanted more for us than what he had.

He truly wanted us to be successful.

While I always loved that about him and Adam's mom, it was not something I was used to.

I will always love them for that.

Adam and I had a great summer chasing girls and bad guys, being accountable to nothing and to no one other than ourselves and our egos. We were barely accountable to the law. We wrote a ton of tickets for ordinance violations and arrested people for almost anything, mostly those who invaded the Jersey Shore for the purpose of fist pumping (BENYS– Bergen or Essex counties, New York and Staten Island). It was known as a "Shore tax." It was kind of like going to the casino and knowing you were likely to lose.

A calculated risk.

In the end, the arrestee would spend the night in the "think tank," a small concrete room lined with narrow benches and O-rings to cuff them until they could see the judge the next morning and pay the "Shore tax."

Ummm ... err ... the "fine."

Working as a part-time cop at the Jersey Shore was a great learning experience. That summer I learned how talented I was at creative writing. I am not saying that I am proud of it. It certainly is not a fair way of conducting business, nor is it an acceptable way of policing, but in the late 90s, that was the reality. I learned how to talk to people without getting my ass kicked.

And yes, there was a learning curve.

I learned how to leverage one experience for another and how to police a population of people who thought cops were a joke but then would have a quick come-to-Jesus moment after we beat the piss out of them and dragged them to jail.

While making an arrest, I learned how to take a punch from the dude who spends 16 hours in the gym every day and the rest of the time eating protein and jacking steroids. I learned that this job was a one-time experience and that for the rest of my career I would have to be an adult and take this shit seriously because "nobody likes you when you're 23 and you still act like you're in freshman year."

Thank you, Blink 182!

CHAPTER FOUR
Daddy Issues

I t is my belief that every young boy should have a father figure in his life. I also believe that the failure and degradation of the nuclear household has led to many of the ills of today's society. Coming from a broken home, myself, I did not allow that to define me. I would not be a statistic or forced into a pattern of behavior as an adult, especially with a family of my own. While carrying the bags of my ancestors, I refuse to carry the baggage.

By all accounts, my father was a real piece of shit. He held an accounting degree from a decent university, but after many attempts, he was never able to pass the CPA exam. He bounced from job to job, and every company he ever worked for went bankrupt. The only professional consistency for my father was his secretary. She followed him to every place of employment, like a package deal. When my parents got divorced, we learned they actually *were* a package deal. They had been romantically involved before, during, and well after my parents were married. She also had a child that looked more like my father than I do.

Hmmm ...

Early on in my life, I was fortunate to recognize that I needed a father figure, and the one I was born from was not it. I had many men to look up to though, and to this day, I try to connect with them all on Father's Day. I am sure to thank them for all that they have done for me throughout my life. Adam's dad, Jack, was certainly one of the most important. He was a cop, and he showed both me and Adam how to be a good dad. He cared for me, like I was one of his own.

There was also Ron, Chuck, Bruce, Bob, Mark, and John. They are the dads of my life-long, college and adult friends. One of them was my boss for a good part of my career. I also include my father-in-law, but he entered my life when I was 27 years old. While he was and is a father figure, for sure, he plays a much different role.

I learned a lot from my bio-dad. I learned to be faithful and committed to my wife. I learned to put my own needs second (or third), behind the needs of my children and my wife. I learned to do everything in the exact opposite way he did it. I learned that I will literally do anything to make sure that my children have a better life than I did. *Note: I said a better life, not an easier life.*

A good life comes from showing gratitude for the things you have. It comes from counting your blessings and not concerning yourself with the things you wish you had. That is not to say you should not set goals and a plan to achieve them. Being grateful will simply give you a spiritual platform to excel and improve your chances of reaching those goals. Having a good life does not mean there will be no challenges or adversity to overcome. It is the challenges and adversities that give you a chance to learn and grow. It is that growth that will elevate you to a life that is good.

My father left our home and family for the fourth and final time in the summer of 1988, shortly after my bar mitzvah. Over the course of many years and fights between my parents, my mom either kicked him out or he left because he knew it was coming. He would be gone for a few days, maybe a week. The longest he was ever away, was about three weeks. I cannot say my folks actually figured things out, but my father would eventually come home. I think they found common ground, enough to tolerate coexisting under the same roof for mine and my sister's sake.

I still have mixed feelings about that.

My parents slept in the same room but separate beds. Mostly, though, my dad slept on the couch downstairs in the basement. They never showed affection, and they never talked to each other. All communication was in the form of yelling or passing notes.

When my father left for good, he did so with purpose. By that, I mean, he did not take a single thing with him. He was cool, calm, and collected, as he exited with a sense of relief and confidence. He clearly had some place to go, some place where he had already established himself. In a way, he appeared to be going home.

Within weeks my mom obtained an attorney, filed for divorce, and spent the rest of my childhood fighting for money my father did not have. She wanted me to have a greater life than she did. My father did not come around much after that, but he was sure to fight for shared custody. Oddly, though, more often than not, he would cancel when we were supposed to see him. It was all good though because my sister and I did not want to see him anyway. However, it still was a bit of a punch in the gut, knowing that our own father did not want to see us.

Over the next 18 months, we adjusted to not having my father around. We saw him on the occasional Sunday, but moved forward with our life, maintaining an obligatory relationship. In the fall of 1989, my sister went off to college. Then it was just me and my mom at home. She did the best she could at raising a teenage boy, getting me through my high school years. I give her much credit for whatever success I have had. While she did not have any confidence in my success, she kept me from getting involved with drugs and other bad influences. She fought for me every time I fucked something up, proving her point that I would most likely be a failure. It was her motherly instinct to protect me. Deep in her heart and soul, I know she wanted the best for me, but she set her bar really low on what success could look like for me.

I did not see my father much, if at all, during my high school years. Honestly, I'm not sure if he even made it to my graduation. Actually, I am pretty sure he did not. The only thing I remember from my high school graduation is the flask I was drinking from in the staging room. The only reason I know I was actually there is because my mom took pictures, and I am in them. Otherwise, I have no recollection. I was not a drunk, and I was not into drugs. However, I was introduced to alcohol and marijuana my sophomore or junior year at Temple Youth Group events—of all places. I learned early on how to self-medicate and calm my anxiety. It was not until a few years later that I learned how much was *too* much.

While in college, I received two letters from my father. The first letter was written while on a trip he took with his common-law wife. It contained a picture of the two of them on a beach, as if I cared to see his lifelong mistress in a bikini. The second piece of correspondence was a postcard with a picture of Hofstra University and a note that read, "I'm in town visiting with family and was hoping to see you. Not sure if I will have time but hoping you can skip class for some lunch."

You would think I would be most disappointed about his priorities, but what really got me was that we had no family on Long Island. I was not sure whose family he was visiting, but it certainly was not mine.

That was my junior year in college, and I did not see or hear from him again until, you guessed it, graduation. My father showed up uninvited and unannounced. I barely knew this man, and I no longer felt comfortable calling him Dad. He was a really old-looking version of the person I remembered but was the same clown I never forgot.

Similar to my high school graduation ceremony, I was anxious and self-medicated. I was surprised that I made it. I saw my father in the crowd before the ceremony started and managed to avoid him.

Afterwards, I was not so lucky.

My mother encouraged me to show some grace and let him say hello, offer his congratulations, and maybe even allow him to show some grace himself. He approached me with purpose, the same purpose I last saw when he walked away years earlier. He began in a scathing tone, accompanied by a wagging finger. He said, "How come it's been so long since you have allowed me to be part of your life? I demand to be a part of your life, starting right now. I am making up for lost time. I deserve that."

This drew attention from others, and I knew I had to respond rather than react. So, with the same purpose that I learned from him, I calmly turned and walked away. That was the last time I ever heard his voice, saw his face, and allowed him to be part of my story. To me, he died that day, and he was buried in a grave of failed relationships. I never mourned him, and I am not sure why. My father did resurface later on in my life. He sent an email to me at work, asking for a kidney.

Yes, you read that right.

I never did get back to him on that. However, he showed up a few months later at the police station, asking for me. He berated the dispatcher, demanding he talk with me because, yes, I owed him a kidney. I happened to be working that night. The dispatcher called me on my cell phone to tell me there was a man in the lobby claiming to be my father and asking for me to share my body parts with him. At first, I laughed, and then I froze.

Holy fuck, this guy was serious!

Needless to say, he was told I was not available and that he was not welcome to return, unless he needed police assistance for any other reason than a transplant.

To date, I still have both my kidneys.

∽

In July 2017, I received a phone call from a doctor at a community hospital in New Jersey. He asked if I was David Berez, the son of Fred Berez. I explained that I was, at least biologically.

"We are estranged and short of a kidney request," I said. "I have not heard from him in 20 years."

The doctor explained that my father was in grave health and was sure to pass in the coming days.

"You are the next of kin listed on his health form," he said.

The worst of it was, I was also listed as his health proxy and estate executor. It was weird to hear that, and there was a part of me that was a little sad, too. After all these years of hating him and ignoring his existence, I was forced to confront it and actually bury and mourn him.

In the coming days, my father died. With the consultation and alignment with my sister, we opted to take responsibility for his remains. I contacted a local funeral home in the town where we grew up and where I still worked. After talking with the funeral director, detailing a lifetime of circumstances and the fact that my father died with more debt than most have in savings, he asked one simple question.

"Was your dad ever in the military?"

"Yes," I replied, curiously.

"No worries," the funeral director smiled. "I got this."

My father was cremated with honors he did not deserve, and he was returned to me in a small box. All costs covered by the United States Army.

Thank you for your service.

Quite frankly, serving his country was the only positive thing he ever did with his life. After his death, I was tasked with cleaning up his end-of-life affairs. It wasn't much, but I had to notify every creditor that they were out whatever amount of money he owed. A few tried to hold me responsible, but I laughed and hung up. I begged them all to sue me and, fortunately, none of them did. The only part of the process that I engaged with face-to-face was the place where he lived. It was an apartment complex dedicated to housing destitute, elderly Jews. I learned a lot from its director, maybe more than I should have.

She explained that Fred was a real asshole, a disgusting mess, and all he ever talked to anyone about was his son who was a police officer. Anytime he felt challenged, he used our "relationship" as a threat. The building director also said that she was terrified to meet me. She suspected the apple did not fall far from the tree, and I would be yet another headache to deal with. She later told me that she was pleasantly surprised. She even called me a "good man" for cleaning up after my father's mess.

There was not much in the apartment. He had a few shirts and a jacket, all of which I remembered from my childhood. There was an old laptop computer, a TV, and his wallet. The wallet contained his social security card, his VA card, and two photographs from the mid 80s—school pictures of my sister and me. She was 14, and I was 10. I imagine that is how he remembered us the rest of his life. There was bloody gauze and dirty underwear scattered about. His place reminded me of the many shitholes I entered as an intern with the New York City Medical Examiner's Office. I always wondered who those scumbags were and who would live like that. Now I know.

They were all my father.

While I wish I had a functional father figure in my home growing up, I want to highlight the father figures I have in my life, the ones I previously noted:

Jack, I always knew that I could come to you with anything, and that there wasn't anything you wouldn't do for me. You and Karen have always had my back and gave me my best friend. You are family to me.

Ron, you were always an inspiration to me. While I first met you as a friend to my parents at Temple services as a little boy, you inspired me to join the rescue squad, become an EMT, and be certified as a rescue technician. You were a badass and a master of the Hurst Tool, and I always strived to be the hero you were to me.

Chuck, you helped with my taxes and finances. As the father of one of my best friends, you gave me guidance and advice as if I was your own.

Bruce, you and Linda took me into your lives as a fourth child. It is because of you I had the great fortune of meeting my wife. I am forever grateful for all that you have done for me.

Bob T., you were a role model throughout my time on the squad and beyond. You believed in me at a time when no one else did. While I think you may have wanted me to be your son-in-law, I was happy to be more of a brother to your daughter. Thank you for always being there for me.

Bob F., your support and friendship over the years has been a link back to the generations before us. You, too, have had unimaginable loss in recent years, and I think of you often.

Mark, you have always looked out for me. You started as the dad of a high school friend, but when I became a cop, you transitioned into a courtroom opponent as a local defense attorney who I always appreciated working with when you represented someone I had arrested... often someone I knew from town. You are always great counsel to me through real estate transactions, wills, and any other legal advice. It is my true honor and privilege to support the Joshua Harr Shane Foundation in honor and memory of your beloved son and show you and the entire family how much we love you too. Your family is my family.

John (Lt.), you were the toughest dude I ever had to work for, but you were fair and always there to teach a life lesson. You led by example, and I always respected you for the man you were and the man you helped me become. I will never forget the day I literally saved your life when you were in anaphylactic shock. While I was so scared to lose you, I was thankful to be in a position to rescue you after a lifetime of you rescuing me. I am so sorry that we lost you while I was writing this book, and you were not able to know how much you meant to my growth.

The lesson here; never forego the chance to tell someone what they mean to you. You don't know if you may ever have the chance again. I am so grateful for the richness, support and guidance these good men brought to my life and livelihood. Without them, I would not be the man, husband, and father I am today.

To you, the reader, I ask that you take pause right now and write a letter of gratitude to someone in your life who has either mentored you, influenced you, loved you, or who has grown apart from you. Write to them, explaining how much they have meant to you. Tell them how much they have inspired you. Tell them how much you love them. If you have their phone number, call and read the letter to them with no explanation. Embrace their reaction and reconnect on the next level. If you cannot call them, mail the letter to them. If they are no longer living, deliver it to them in a prayer. You will not regret this exercise.

While I have written the "gratitude letter" during a resiliency training course, I need to write an apology in these pages to my three children—Alex, Zack, and Danielle. You have all asked about my father, your grandfather, during your respective elementary and middle school years. I told all three of you the same lie when you asked individually. I told you he died when I was young, and he was not a good man. I also told you that there was nothing of value to know about him, and I know that has left you all with more questions than answer. However, you never asked anything about him again. You saw the pain in my heart and chose to protect me over satisfying your own needs for understanding. I love the three of you more than you will ever know. While I believed I was protecting you from him, in reality, it was you protecting me from my Daddy issues. I apologize for lying to you, and I promise to do better.

CHAPTER FIVE
Day One

I n September of 1999, my time as a special police officer with the Seaside Park Police Department was coming to an end. The summer was over. The BENYS were all headed home to recover from three months of fist pumping, excessively loud club music, an overindulgence of boardwalk pizza, and the worst beer on the planet. Being a beach cop in New Jersey was my first step to a full-time career in law enforcement and the place where many of us got our start. I had set myself on a journey and was in the process of taking tests and applying to any agency that was hiring.

The late 90s and into the 2000s, law enforcement was still a sought-after career, and job opportunities were limited. Base salaries were on the rise. Benefits were top-notch and after 10 years of service, an officer could make as much money as their well-established peers in the business world. While the financials were modernizing, the hiring process was lagging. It was still a bit of a "good ol' boys" system, and you had to know the right people or at least know people who knew people. Police work is a business of trust, a fraternity of legacy, and if you did not come with some level of *street cred*, it was difficult to break in.

My application to become a full-time police officer with the East Windsor Police Department was completed, submitted, and under consideration. I spent several years getting to that moment, having the ability to fill in all the blanks that would not only qualify me but allow me to be considered for the job. I was a 10-year volunteer with the local rescue squad. I received a bachelor's degree from a great university. I completed a one-of-a-kind internship, graduated from the police academy, and proved my ability to do the job while working at the Seaside Park Police Department. While nothing in life happens without "knowing someone," I can honestly say that I authentically created these relationships on my own and developed my worthiness, accountability, and loyalty.

The application was approximately 30 pages. I still have a copy of it in my filing cabinet. If there is anything anyone ever wanted to know about me, from the day I was born to the day I filled it out, it is in that document. Completing the application was a daunting task, not because it was time consuming or because I had to generate supporting documents for much of the information. It was because I was faced with my life's decisions and having to account for my relationships, everyone I was ever close to—past and present. Those 30 pages contain the good, the bad, and the ugly of every part of my life. Quite frankly, it was the first time I was forced to face many of my demons, at least the ones I had up to that point.

After the application was submitted, I had a one-on-one with the chief of police. He was an old-school guy and knew me as the local kid who wanted to be a cop. East Windsor was a small town, a bit frozen in time, and the chief all but offered me a job on the spot without even seeing if I spelled my own name correctly on the application. I cannot believe I spent two months of my life preparing that thing, and he never even looked at it. He gave the standard lecture about police work, expressing his expectations of me. He also told me that hiring me would be his last official act as chief because he was retiring in six weeks. He made mention that the guy who was promoted into his position really did not care for me. He said, "If I don't hire you now, he won't. Oh, and good luck with your career. That guy really hates you."

While the chief was ready for me to start immediately, I still needed to have my background check completed by an agency detective, confirming all that I had noted in my application. The detective was a great guy, and I would come to respect him as a police officer, supervisor, and friend. By the end of the investigation, he would know more about me than I would know about myself. He spoke with my mom, my sister, my brother-in-law, a few friends, and some ex-girlfriends. During the post background interview, the detective asked, "Have you ever pissed anyone off? I could not find one single person to say one bad thing about you, not even your ex-girlfriend's brother."

I smiled, as the detective continued, "Honestly, that guy finds you so fascinating. I can't believe he literally wrote about you in his book and then titled the book the same as the poem he wrote in your image. Pretty cool."

I just sat there and smiled, thinking to myself, I am glad he could not find my father and, clearly, he did not speak to any of my high school teachers or college professors. They would have, for sure, had me disqualified.

So, on December 7, 1999, at the Township Council meeting and in the presence of family, friends, Township residents, and future colleagues, I was sworn into the East Windsor Police Department as Patrol Officer David Uri Berez—Badge #64.

This *was the proudest moment of my life.*

Another "*fuck you*" moment to all those who never believed in me and did not think I had what it took to be successful, let alone have the strength, courage, and wisdom to become a police officer.

For all of her negativity, fear, and discontent regarding my decision to journey down this path, I believe that this was one of *the* proudest days for my mother as well. I know this is not what she wanted for me and my career. I know that she was scared of the risk I was taking—mentally and physically. I know that seeing me in a uniform was a stark reminder of my father, the juxtaposition between the awe-inspiring moment she met her knight in shining armor and the evil human he turned out to be. Moreover, I know it was at that moment she let go of me … her child.

It was an evening of celebration. It was the tip of the spear for all the hard work that led up to this moment of accomplishment, but it was also "Day One" of the rest of my life. It was the transition from my youth to adulthood, from citizen to police officer, from victim to victor.

After the ceremony, we had cake at police headquarters, and I was able to take my family and friends on a tour of the station. They were able to see the place I would spend the next 20 years of my life and have a bit of a connection to the job, the stories I would tell, and the men and women standing to my right and to my left while serving our community.

Over the course of my career, I worked with many different types of people, cops who joined the force for many different types of reasons. I could have easily been of the mindset, like a few of them, that I was going to get back at the world for all the wrong the world had done to me. I could have been like others and arrest those who bullied me. I could take advantage of girls who ignored me. I could even punish those who represented folks who had wronged me. However, I chose a higher, purpose-filled path to give back to a community that saved me and to protect the officers who protected me. I chose to serve as a role model for kids who did not already have one.

I was going to save the world.

The celebration ended, and with some gleeful anxiety, I went home for a good night of sleep. It was the best I would ever have. It was my last night as a kid in my mother's house, my last night in my childhood bed, and my last night as David. It was a lot to take in. I thought to myself, "Tomorrow will be my first full day as Officer Berez."

Day one.

⤜

I showed up to work wearing a suit, as I had not yet been issued a uniform or equipment. I was introduced to everyone at the station, learning who played what role in the department, what their rank was, and how they wanted to be addressed. I was finally fitted for a uniform. I signed a ton of paperwork. I was presented with my official badge and identification cards and then handed a five-inch binder of policy and procedure. I was told to sit in the basement and read through and memorize the materials so that I could be tested at the end of the day.

So much for saving the world on day one.

It took me three days (with a few breaks in between) just to get through the binder. During the breaks, I qualified with the department-issued firearms, certified with OC spray, reviewed handcuffing techniques, and certified with the PR-24 side-handled baton.

I was becoming a regular badass.

For those not familiar with OC spray, it is law enforcement's version of pepper spray. While any civilian can pick up a keychain-style version at Walmart, a police officer must go through four hours of training, take a written test, and be sprayed with it in order to be able to carry it on the job. Not only were we given an excessive dose of the Oleoresin Capsicum (OC) cocktail that makes your eyes feel like they are burning through your skull and cause a waterfall of mucus to evacuate from every opening in your body, but you are simultaneously attacked by your instructors, having to fight them off while battling the effects of the OC. It was true entertainment for all those who came to watch.

*And trust me, **everyone** comes to watch.*

It is great training though. I can't even count how many times I was inadvertently sprayed by my colleagues over the years while fighting with a suspect. It often happens when an officer uses the spray to subdue a shitbag.

My in-service training was complete. I was assigned to a field training officer. For the purpose of this story, we will call my FTO, Skippy. Skippy and I were friends before I got hired. As I was "networking" through the years, I had gone out to bars and clubs with several of the officers from the department. The most notable were Skippy, Bart and Joe. I was like their little brother. They went out of their way to include me in their clique.

Skippy spoke with a nasally tone and presented himself exactly as you would picture a 25-year-old cop from the 90s—blond, muscular build, flat-top haircut, and dark sunglasses. I was pleasantly surprised to learn how knowledgeable he was and how he was able to talk to people.

And the guy never lost a foot chase.

He was, by all accounts, one of *the* best cops I ever had the pleasure to work with and learn from. Skippy was a hard charger and worked every hour of overtime he could. He had a sixth sense of where to find trouble, and he always stepped in shit.

I loved it!

He also knew exactly how far to push the legal envelope so that we could effectively do our job without getting jammed up and still have fun doing it. He was like the Howard Stern of police work, back in the day when Howard was still on regular radio. I was a sponge during the FTO phase. I took in as much as I could. As a police officer, you never stop learning. You never stop growing, and you must *always* be willing to adapt and overcome. FTO was likely one of my favorite parts of my career. I had never worked harder, never made more mistakes, and never grew as much as I did in those three months before being released from the coach program and set out on my own. Transition complete!

Welcome to the world, Police Officer Berez #64.

CHAPTER SIX
Switching to Guns

I n the early 2000s, policing was a fairly benign sport, running below the radar in most people's lives. The 90's drug war was slowing down; social media did not yet exist; Google just launched, and the Motorola StarTAC was the latest and greatest in cell phone technology. It did not have picture-taking capability, so cops were able to do their jobs without being micromanaged by the uneducated and uninformed public.

I should note, I am 100 percent for accountability, just not selective accountability through out-of-context video clips used to fit a personal, political, or media narrative. If you want to share a story, share the whole story.

Our agency was split into four patrol squads, two on days and two on nights. We rotated every 28 days which was just long enough to get acclimated to that side of the clock before switching back. Most of the time we were walking zombies. I enjoyed working the night shift (1800 hours to 0600 hours) because if shit was gonna happen, it usually happened at night. Not to knock our agency, but as a whole, it was a bit archaic when it came to the tools of the trade. We did not have Mobile Data Terminals—MDTs (in-car computers). We did not have personal computers in the station. We worked off a Unix-based system with dummy terminals (green screens). Our uniforms resembled the Dukes of Hazard's Sheriff Rosco P. Coltrain, and our leather was basketweave to match the 70's motif.

Speaking of leather, we wore shined chukka boots and a level-one gun holster with no retention. We looked like we just walked in the 1979 Memorial Day Parade, minus the American flag on our uniform. Those were removed after 9/11 (of all times) when a resident complained about the look of the subdued gray flag against the gray uniform shirt. It was never replaced during my career.

One warm Friday night in late June, I was off FTO, working with Skippy, Bart, Shaky Jake, Cap, Jumbo, and Stock. Stock was our sergeant. (*Note to reader: These nicknames are to protect the identity of the actual guys in my squad.*) We, along with two other folks in our unit who were not socially relatable, were a relatively tight group. Our patrol squad was a group of misfits who did great police work but who often used unconventional and certainly more creative methods to complete the task at hand—none of which were illegal. We were not paper pushers, good report writers, students of policy and procedure, or ass kissers. We were common-sense, knuckle draggers who only "asked once" for compliance. And because of our reputation, we only had to ask once.

We were unconventional, for sure, but we got shit done.

That night, it was business as usual. There were a variety of car stops, DUI arrests, a few calls for service and the regular juveniles running about in the apartment complex, creating a less than awesome quality of life for others.

At about 11 o'clock, we received a radio call for a disturbance in the area of Princeton Arms South 2, a garden-style apartment complex where disturbances commonly occurred. The dispatcher advised that the caller believed there was a male and a female arguing, and the male had a knife. So, the call quickly went from an annoyed neighbor to a domestic violence incident with a weapon. The dispatcher came back a little later, informing the responding officers that the knife was actually a sword, and the suspect was dressed in a black trench coat. He had long, black hair and was known to the caller as A%& M#$$#&.

For the purposes of this story, we will call our suspect Abe.

Abe was well known to the police. The department considered him a "regular." He was a local, goth kid whose behavior was definitely a concern. If a situation was ever to escalate, we thought he might eventually hurt someone. Over time, he was growing to be a greater and greater threat.

Upon arrival, I immediately recognized Abe. He ran swiftly into the woods when he saw Skippy and me. We gave chase as other responding officers stood by with the victim. Abe ran away with the sword in hand and was known to fight the police when caught. So, I was sure of two things: Firstly, I was going to catch the little turd, and secondly, one of us was going to get hurt in the process. As we were running through the woods, my gear was bouncing around; my vest was too tight, making it hard to breath, and I did not know those woods well enough to properly call out waypoints or our final location when we did eventually catch the fucker. Skippy tackled Abe with the sword in hand and directed me to hold him at gunpoint while he secured the weapon and put Abe into handcuffs. I went to draw my gun from the holster, and I immediately knew something was not right. The thumb break was not snapped, and the holster was, well, empty.

Holy Shit! My gun was gone!

For those of you who are not police officers, the act of drawing your weapon takes less than a second when you are properly trained. For that particular holster, it was a four-part process completed in one motion.

Release the thumb break.

Drive the web of your hand into the backstrap.

Grasp the stock/grip.

Pull straight up to draw.

That "less than a second" went into slow motion as each one of those steps brought me closer to the realization my gun was gone. I did not outwardly react, but I was most certainly in dire panic. It was dark. We were in the woods, and there was no one but me, Skippy, and Abe. Without missing a beat, I drew my expandable baton, otherwise known as an ASP, and held it like a gun. Abe complied with all Skippy's orders and was secured without incident. Skippy helped Abe to his feet and looked over at me, as if to acknowledge a job well done. He saw me pointing my ASP like a gun. His expression went from "Good job, kid!" to "What the fuck?"

"I lost my gun," I whispered.

Now, Skippy and I were both in panic mode, and Abe … well, he laughed all the way back to the patrol car. I will say this, the low hanging tree branches were pretty humbling for Abe. Not sure how, but he managed to "find" every one of them with his forehead.

Abe was secured in Shakey's patrol car to be transported back to the station for processing. This would ordinarily be done by the arresting officer, but Skippy and I had to find my lost gun.

Holy crap! I still feel the stress of that moment.

While I always believed in the model of *Extreme Ownership,* long before New York Times Bestselling Author Jocko Willink wrote the book on "taking ownership of everything in his domain, including the outcome and everything that affects it," I will note that this incident was not completely my fault. I did note earlier, our leather gear was not the best, nor was it tactically appropriate.

We wore parade-ready gear, not battle-ready gear. We were destined for failure, but at least we would look good failing. Our level—

one holster had no retention built in, and the thumb-break strap was the only part that prevented the gun from bouncing out. On a new holster, like mine, it was issued with the strap having never been bent over and snapped to the other side. So, even when the strap *was* snapped over the gun, the leather naturally wanted to return to a straightened position, causing a ton of stress on the cheaply constructed snap.

During the foot chase, the snap opened, the strap released, and my gun bounced out like a loaded baby kangaroo from its mother's pouch. Skippy and I, along with Bart and Jumbo, traced our steps from the patrol car back through the woods, in the direction of the recent foot chase. By some miracle, we located my gun after about 30 minutes. I was incredibly relieved, but I knew that would not be the end of the story. I would have to document the incident. It was my introduction to Internal Affairs, and my Seaside Park experience in creative writing would suddenly come in handy. When I asked the more senior officers in my squad how to best approach this, I will never forget the prophetic words and advice of Jumbo. I would hear these words many times throughout my career.

"Never happened, bro."

I actually thought about his "advice" and considered avoiding the situation, like it actually never happened. However, I saw this as a situation bigger than me. It was something so much more than just a single incident with shitty equipment and a guaranteed Internal Affairs complaint. I saw it as an opportunity to own the failure and present it as an opportunity to fix a problem that many had complained about for years but never had a situation to confirm their fears—at least none that was reported.

"Good!"

For the rest of you Jocko fans, you get the reference.

"Failure is just an opportunity to improve."

After completing the arrest and investigation reports, I drafted a special report regarding the lost and found, department-issued service weapon and faulty holster. I annotated the problem, described the result of the failure, and offered a solution so that this would never happen to anyone else ever again. Due to my approach of "extreme ownership" and offering a solution to a known problem, I avoided the IA complaint and opened up a discussion.

The police chief at the time, however, was not as receptive to my solution as I had hoped. When I asked why he was apprehensive about a new holster, I was given the most defeating answer ever. He said, "That's the one we are going to use because that is the holster we have always used, and I personally hand selected it." In other words, that's the way we do it because that's the way we've always done it.

It was the epitome of a fixed mindset.

While he was not willing to make this easy, he did leave room for discussion when he punted the idea back to the rank and file, the union members. One of the officers, who I will refer to as Klammy, was a self-proclaimed tactical expert. He was 5'9, around 425 pounds, and anything but solid muscle. Klammy read every tactical book known at the time and attended every tactical conference he could get to. He was up to date on the latest and greatest of everything with the exception of self-care and nutrition. Klammy was passionate though, and he was all over this new holster idea.

After months of research, Klammy put together a five-page paper, outlining three separate holsters. The paper and holsters were presented to the chief, who reluctantly accepted it and later told Klammy how impressed he was with the way it was put together. The chief chose a new triple-retention holster that was the latest and greatest, and within a few weeks every officer in our department was issued one and trained with it to proficiency. This was a big step for an agency bound to the old way of doing things. While this change in duty holster may not seem like a big deal to the average person and may not even have been a big deal to other police officers within our agency, it was life changing to me. While it was important to me that I was able to facilitate positive change within the agency, especially considering it stemmed from something that was ultimately my fault, this new holster literally saved my life.

∽

It was about one o'clock on a Saturday morning, approximately one year after receiving our new safety holsters. I was driving eastbound on Route 33, through the Twin Rivers section of East Windsor. I observed the illuminated taillights of a vehicle in an apartment complex parking lot adjacent to the highway. I also observed that there were no headlights, which meant there was someone in the car with their foot on the brake. I entered the lot in blackout mode, meaning I turned off my vehicle lights, inside and out. I parked a short but visible distance from the suspicious vehicle. I say "suspicious" because there is no legitimate reason for an individual to be sitting in a parked vehicle at 1 a.m.

My experience told me that there would be drugs, alcohol, sexual solicitation or a domestic dispute related to the occupied vehicle. I approached the parked car. However, from a distance, no one was visible from the outside. When I reached the car, I saw two men reclined on the front seats. I also detected a strong odor of an alcoholic beverage through the open window. I recognized the front-seat passenger as a 19-year-old named Chris. He was a local pain in the ass who was always fighting with his parents and younger brother. Chris had a bottle of brandy between his legs and was visibly intoxicated. I directed him to exit the vehicle, but he refused to do so. In an effort to avoid escalation of the situation, I turned to the driver. The guy in the driver's seat, whose name escapes me, complied with my request and exited the vehicle.

For officer safety, it is prudent to only have one subject exit the vehicle at a time. I was vigilant about this procedure but always prepared if the occupants called an audible on me. With the driver out of the car, Chris decided to use that to his advantage by also getting out and swiftly making a break on foot, attempting to run away. I ran after him, leaving the otherwise compliant driver behind. I radioed to dispatch that I was in a foot pursuit. Chris only got about 50 yards before I caught up to him and jacked him up against the side of my marked patrol car. I ordered him to submit to arrest, but he had other plans.

While arresting him, Chris verbalized that there was no way he was going back to jail. He said, "I'll kill you first!" He had just spent six months in prison for a domestic violence charge he received after punching his mom, causing injury to her face. It was clear to me that he had spent the majority of that six-month "vacation" in the gym. He was definitely stronger than me and much more prepared for the fight than I was.

During the struggle, Chris punched me in the face with a closed fist, trying to knock me out. We continued to engage in a physical altercation, which seemed like it went on for hours. I could hear sirens in the distance; they were getting closer with every passing moment. I was taking a beating from this jailhouse rat, but I was not going to give up. Everything about my experience in the police academy was being put to good use. The pain would only be temporary; losing would be permanent.

Losing was not an option.

Chris grabbed for my handgun and vigorously attempted to remove it from the holster. I was able to utilize the weapon retention technique of lifting from the bottom of the holster and pushing my gun into my waist. While this was successful in retaining control of my gun, it limited my fighting to one hand. I was losing pretty badly and was afraid that he would, indeed, try to kill me. He had already verbalized it and then tried to get my gun.

At that point, I felt I had probable cause to use deadly force to eliminate the threat to my own life. I changed my mindset, as well as my physical objective to unholstering my weapon and shooting Chris. It was like in the 1986 movie Top Gun when Maverick was in a dog fight, and he said, "Goose, switching to guns."

I made several attempts to unholster my gun but was not able to do it. I was so fucking pissed off that this new holster was so difficult to manipulate. I thought I might actually get killed in the process of trying to get to my gun. While in the heat of the struggle, I verbalized to Chris that I was going to shoot him. Chris suddenly disengaged from the fight and ran towards the woods. I started to chase after him, unsuccessfully attempting to draw my weapon. I did not chase too far, as the Calvary was arriving on scene. The driver was placed into protective custody while two other officers chased after Chris. He was apprehended about 15 minutes later by my squad mates. He had suffered a few broken fingers from my weapon retention maneuver and some other minor injuries that supposedly resulted from the subsequent arrest. That's still debatable, as the report reads: "Never happened, bro!"

I suffered a sprained wrist and a bruised ego that night, but I later learned that I also suffered a broken holster. This new holster saved my life. When Chris first attempted to disarm me for the purpose of using my own gun against me, his attempt at a reverse draw broke the retention mechanism (as the holster is designed to do) and locked the weapon in place. This was an unknown feature that we had not trained for. This feature is specifically designed to allow the officer to fight with both hands without concern for weapon retention. What a gift this technology is. My agency still uses this holster to this day.

Klammy left the department not too long after that incident. He suffered from narcolepsy and had a propensity for lying, neither of which is conducive to a successful law enforcement career. However, I will forever be grateful to him and his research that led us to this new holster. It may not have seemed like much at the time, but it literally saved my life.

Chris was charged with attempting to disarm a police officer with the intent to kill. He did 10 years in prison and was killed in a drug deal a few weeks after his release.

As for me, while I was still pretty new at the job, I had so many varied experiences, many of which were reported in local media. I would no longer be David Berez ever again. I would forever be known in my own community as Officer Berez. I had hit that pivot point of no return. There is a very important lesson in this story, and that is always do what is right, even if it may be at your own peril. It *did* happen, bro!

Own it!

And like Jocko teaches, use adversity as an opportunity to grow. I would also encourage police leaders to remember that their rank does not always make them the smartest person in the room. Oftentimes, those closest to a situation may have better working knowledge than you. So, trust your people to know what works best, and more importantly, what doesn't. Lastly, and most important of all, always keep fighting. Backup will always arrive. You won't fail unless you quit.

Don't quit!

CHAPTER SEVEN
September 10, 2001

T hroughout my life, I spent a lot of time in New York City. Where I grew up, worked, and currently live in Central New Jersey is about 50 miles southwest of the City. My family has a soft spot in our heart for New York, as it was the open-armed welcome where my mother's parents and grandparents arrived in this country, following their emigration from Nazi occupied Germany. While most of my family found their way to the suburbs of New Jersey, my Aunt Edith remained a single New Yorker her entire life, until she passed away in early 2002.

Edith lived in a single room occupancy (SRO) apartment in the Windermere Hotel at 666 West End Avenue. She rented there from the time she was 18 years old in the summer of 1943. It was our family's routine to take the Suburban Bus from East Brunswick, New Jersey to the Port Authority Bus Depot on 42nd Street every other Sunday to meet Aunt Edith in the City. We would go to Horn and Hardart's (automat) for lunch, then window shop at Macy's and, on special occasions, we would see a show on Broadway.

For those who remember New York City in the 1980s, I got a real-time education about sex and drugs when traversing 42nd Street or Times Square. I vividly remember the look on my mom's face when I asked, "What is a peep show?" I was going to ask her for a quarter, so I could look in the window, but I quickly realized the "peep show" had nothing to do with dancing marshmallow bunnies.

I had grown to love New York, and that passion solidified through my college years on Long Island, which was only a 25-minute train ride away. I enjoyed all that the City offered, especially the year I was an intern with the New York City Medical Examiner's Office. I suppose that is why over the course of 72 hours in September of 2001, that passion turned me into a protector and a rescuer of a place that was home to me. That same passion turned to sadness and anger and then to fear and post-traumatic stress responses.

It was 1800 hours on Monday, September 10, 2001. I was starting my last nightshift of the set. It was a perfect fall evening, a cool, dry night with nothing on the agenda. School was back in session, so there were no kids running about town. Half the bars and restaurants were closed, and the other half shut down early. Monday night shift was generally quiet except for the regular Monday night domestic calls that usually resulted from weekend baby-mama drama. This particular Monday night was no different. I made a few traffic stops before the sun set and cruised quietly through the rest of the shift.

As my squad ended the workday at 0600 hours on the morning of September 11th, we unloaded our patrol cars, secured our equipment, and headed down to the locker room to change out of our uniforms and into our civilian clothes. With some regular morning banter, we walked out the back door of the police station, got into our personal cars, and headed home to go to sleep. Little did we know, at the exact same time, there was evil lurking just a few miles away, as would-be terrorists were just arriving at Newark Airport.

How could we have known the significance of the night before when a friend in a neighboring agency stopped a man named Mohamad Atta and issued him a motor vehicle summons for an expired license and sent him on his way? Or that a local resident and would-be hero, Todd Beemer, was leaving Cranbury, New Jersey to go on a business trip?

Let's Roll!

Who could have known that three other East Windsor residents would show up to work at the World Trade Center for the last time and never make it home?

To one of those residents, Mr. Lai, I tried so very hard to mentor your son after you were gone, but I was not able to get through to him. He was just not able to manage life without you. I am so sorry.

To this day, I always wonder if they kissed their family members goodbye that morning or if they said I love you. Did they hold a door for someone on the commute or did someone give them a smile that made them feel good? Was their last act one of kindness, even in the shadows of evil?

I arrived home at around 0650 hours and had a bowl of cereal before heading to bed. I remember that moment vividly because I never ate when I got home from the nightshift. However, I would usually have a beer (or six!) to assist my ability to fall asleep, so I could overcome the rising sun, the sound of garbage pickup, and the morning commuters. For those who have never worked a nightshift and tried to go to sleep while the rest of the world is revving their engines, cutting their lawn, returning your email, and making follow-up phone calls, please don't judge the 7 a.m. beers. It is not only common but also a 100-percent necessary evil.

On this day, however, something was different. I felt different, but not in a way you would think. I was relaxed. I was calm, and I was at peace on that cool, still, blue-sky morning. I wanted to enjoy the solace of the moment with clarity and without the numbing effect of the alcohol.

Who knew?

I lived alone in my two-bedroom townhouse, except for the occasional overnight guest. I went up to my room, washed my face, changed my clothes, and climbed into bed. My bedroom windows were open to let in the fresh air, and my blackout shades were left open, so I could stare out the window and enjoy the clear, crisp sky. While I generally would have turned on the TV and drifted off into an alcohol-supported slumber to an episode of Family Guy, this day was different. I embraced the moment and slowly and consciously fell asleep. My brain was unusually still, and for the first time in a long time, I did not have any dreams.

The next thing I remember was my phone ringing. It is important to note that in September of 2001, cell phone use was still an emerging technology with wireless plans being expensive and charging by the minute. No one called your cell phone unless they knew you were not home, or the call was important enough to warrant the $.10 per minute. On this particular morning, the ringing was coming from my cell phone. The sound woke me from a deep, REM sleep—startling me. No one in their right mind would call my cell phone at 0911 hours.

Yes, you read the right—9:11 a.m., following a midnight shift.

As you know, nothing good ever comes from an unexpected, early morning call, particularly when everyone knows you are sleeping. Anyone with my cell phone number was close enough to me to know my sleep schedule.

The caller ID on the Nokia 5110 display read my sister's new home phone number in Charlottesville, Virginia. My sister and I have always been very close. There is not a single day in our lives, then or now, that one of us would not answer the phone when the other is calling. This has served two objectives. The first being, we are there to share in each other's joys. Secondly, we are always there to support each other in a time of need. This closeness has saved us from panic because when you don't stay connected, getting a phone call at this hour could only mean one thing—bad news.

My sister was a hospital nurse who, like me, worked rotating shifts, so we purposely shared our schedules out of respect for each other's sleep hours. So, when the phone rang, and I saw it was her, I answered. I knew it was not going to be good news.

"Hello," I said with a crusty voice.

"Are you watching the news," my sister asked in an anxious tone.

"Are you fucking kidding me right now," I replied. "You know I worked last night, and you want to know if I'm watching the news?"

My sister paused, so as to collect herself. "Listen to me," she sighed. "Open your eyes, take a deep breath, and turn on the news. You need to see what is going on and check in with work. I love you." So many thoughts went through my head in about an eighth of a second.

Was one of my guys shot this morning?

Did it make the news?

But wait, she said, "I love you."

Was I shot last night?

Did I not make it?

Was this one of those weird cop death dreams?

What the fuck is happening right now?

CHAPTER EIGHT
9/11

fter I realized I was both awake and alive, I quickly and somewhat reluctantly collected myself. I turned on the television and ... holy fucking shit!!!!

At first, I thought it was a "War of the Worlds" type of broadcast. After all, I did grow up down the road from Grover's Mill, a small farm in West Windsor, New Jersey where Orson Wells claimed the Martians were landing. But in all seriousness, as the seconds and minutes passed, I realized the Martians were actually terrorists. They were crashing, but instead of a farm, they had crashed into the Twin Towers of downtown Manhattan's World Trade Center.

This was the war of the worlds in real time.

I was frozen and speechless. My sister started to cry, apologizing for waking me.

"I thought you should know," she said.

While accepting her apology, I thanked her for calling. I told her that I should get dressed and get back into work. There was another silent pause, and for the first time in a long time, I uttered the words "I love you," words that rarely, if ever, passed my lips. I was not one who ever really knew how to love, not even myself, especially since becoming a cop. It would be days before I talked to my sister again.

As I was getting dressed, I had a quick snack and put together a bag of stuff that I thought I might need. Then, I called my mom. We weren't exactly on speaking terms, but I wanted to make sure she was okay. She was crying and did not have much to say. I explained to her that I was good but would be heading back to work. I was sure we would be getting deployed as a means of support to whatever the hell was going on. My mom begged me not to go, in the same way she begged me not to become a police officer. She said, "Even if you survive, you will never be the same. This will change who you are forever."

Truer words have never been spoken.

Fortunately, I'm still here, but 9/11 did change me. It changed the entire world. I did not respond to her comment but rather said (for the second time in five minutes) the words, "I love you."

It was likely the first time I said those words to her, at least as an adult, and it would be days before we spoke again. I got into my car with bags full of gear and drove as fast as I could back to the station. I pulled into the rear lot of police headquarters, backed into a parking space, and saw my partner, John, entering into the lot as well. John and I looked at each other and had a silent conversation. We had grown very close over the years and did not need the use of words to communicate. We knew why we were both there. We were going to do our part to save the world or whatever was left of it.

We immediately began to develop a plan, all while gathering additional equipment and readying ourselves for a coordinated department deployment. The agency I worked for always demanded an unreasonable level of "perceived excellence," not only during regular shifts but on training days and special assignments as well. It often created angst because it seemed like the brass was more concerned with the appearance of things rather than the actions themselves.

After coordinating our equipment, John and I walked into the station and went directly to the patrol commander's office. John had a few years on me, but we were both young, full of fervor, and ready to go.

⇒   Uniforms squared away

⇒   Equipment self-inspected

⇒   Plan in hand

We knocked on the lieutenant's open door. He stared back at us with a confused, annoyed, and almost pissed-off look. Thinking about it now, makes me laugh. That was his usual response anytime anyone knocked on his door. The lieutenant had an open-door policy, but we all knew what that meant—*my door is **always** open, but it doesn't mean you can come in and bother me.*

"Aren't you two midnights," the lieutenant asked.

"Yes, sir!"

"Then what the fuck are you doing in my office at 10 a.m.?"

"I am sure you have been watching the news this morning, sir. There is a bit of an emergency going on in New York at the moment," I said in a sarcastic tone.

He advised us that he was well aware.

"The United States is under attack, and we are going to war. We are here to do our part," John said. "What's the plan to deploy to New York and support the rescue?"

Then came the simplest, strongest, and most disappointing response. "Not our city, not our problem."

Typical response from the isolationists that ran our agency and town. John and I were stunned, confused, and utterly disappointed. However, we were not surprised. This was the canned response for anything outside the borders of our town. It is important to note that many of the officers I worked with had never even been to New York City. Yes,

58

we were 50 miles south of the greatest city on planet Earth, and yet most of these folks had never been there.

I considered New York City my second home, a place where I spent every other weekend growing up. I went to college there, and I worked there as an intern. Most of the people I worked with in East Windsor were from south of the border. No, not the famous stop in South Carolina or even the country south of the Rio Grande, but rather a defining line through this great state.

New Jersey is split across the center, creating two substates–North Jersey and South Jersey. Route 195 is the demilitarization zone (DMZ), separating pork roll from Taylor ham, hoagies from heroes, Soprano's from Mummers, and New York from Philadelphia. So, when the lieutenant said, "Not our city, not our problem," it was not just a department-wide position on providing mutual aid, it was a personal insult to both John and me, as we both grew up north of New Jersey's own Mason-Dixon line. This was our city. So, we backed out of the office and quietly walked out of the building.

John and I packed up my personal car with our go bags and other personal equipment, changed our clothes to PBA attire (union logo instead of department logo), and headed north. Our agency was overprotective in how it was represented. If you weren't "on the clock," no officer was allowed to wear clothing that represented the agency. If you wanted to show your police pride, it was imperative that you did so through your membership to the police union, the Policemen's Benevolent Association (PBA). There was nothing that the department could do to regulate that.

John and I drove out of the parking lot and headed across town to the New Jersey Turnpike, which runs north and south. We approached the Exit 8 toll booth in East Windsor and found that it was not occupied by an attendant. This was before the creation of EZ Pass. We didn't know it, but all toll road attendants had been pulled from their posts for safety reasons, and the roads were running wide open.

Once we merged onto the highway, my 1998 Honda Passport was put to the test, as we dropped the hammer, traveling at triple digits. We got to Exit 14B in Jersey City in record time. In case you are wondering, the speedometer on the car topped out at 110 mph, and the needle was buried. Clearly, 110 was more of a suggestion, rather than the actual top speed that the car could travel. I can say with full confidence, we exceeded Honda's "suggestion."

As we exited the turnpike, there were local checkpoints, like you would see in war-torn countries controlled by an invading force. John and I ID'd ourselves to the officers and federal agents manning the checkpoints, and they directed us to a small marina in the tourist area of Jersey City. This marina was more of a seaport for local commuters traveling across the Hudson River between New Jersey and New York. Up to that point, Jersey City was a shadow town of New York City with a troubled urban center. Along the shoreline, however, were luxury high-rises facing Manhattan. Most of the residents were young people working in the financial industry—Wall Street and the World Financial Center. So many of them never returned home that day.

As we entered the marina parking lot, a Jersey City police officer directed us to an open space. We moved quickly, as the FDNY fireboat was prepared to get underway. We each grabbed our go bags and ran to the water's edge. A dock attendant was waving his arms, and people were yelling from the boat, "Come on, guys! Let's go!"

My feet hadn't even touched the deck when the boat pushed back. The operator moved ahead at full throttle, but the five-minute ride across the Hudson River felt more like hours. There was a part of me that wished we would freeze in time and never get there. I had never been that scared, not even while on patrol at work when I lost my gun in a foot chase or when a 19-year-old tried to disarm and kill me.

This was the fear of the unknown.

We did not know the other people on the boat, and they certainly did not know us. It turned out, though, they were also off-duty cops running into the fire, while every-day citizens were running away from it. Why would anyone run towards danger like this? Because that's what cops do.

Service and dedication to the preservation of life above all else!

As we crossed the river, the billowing smoke was getting clearer and clearer, but the ground-level view grew hazier and hazier. There was still ash hovering over lower Manhattan, and the smoke from the pile was drifting south through the clear blue sky. It was a dichotomy of atmospheric environments that the human brain could not reconcile. This was not something even the most creative minds in Hollywood could dream up.

As we got closer to the Manhattan shoreline, I could smell death in the air. Death was a smell that I knew all too well from my time on the rescue squad, at the medical examiner's office, and as a cop. Death has a unique aroma, but this was different. I could smell the evil of the terrorists permeating American soil, and I could see its impact in the fright of the victims, the despair of the rescuers, and the sadness of those waiting for loved ones at home, not knowing if they were dead or alive.

CHAPTER NINE
Ground Zero

T he boat docked on the New York side of the Hudson River in the North Cove Marina. This area was well known to recreation boaters; it hosted a sailing school and was a commuter drop zone for those who traveled into the City by ferry for work. The fire boat pushed up against the dock with the engines producing enough thrust so that we could easily step off because there was no one to tie off the dock lines. As soon as we disembarked, many citizens looking to escape to New Jersey jumped on board to be shuttled to safety. For every one of us jumping off of the fireboat, there were 10 jumping on. People were running scared, looking to escape disaster. It was not lost on my partner and I that we were about to run into hell, a hell that everyone else was trying to escape. It was right then I had to ask myself, "Was this a one-way boat ride?"

In the world of emergency services, there are systems in place for large-scale events called the Incident Command System (ICS) and the National Incident Management System (NIMS). This command infrastructure can be used from multi-vehicle crashes to the most horrific, large-scale event you can imagine. These processes have been proven successful over and over again, and as a first responder you come to rely on them for command and control. So, responding to this incident should have been no different. It would be expected that a member of an outside agency would respond to a command center, receive an assignment, and get after that mission. When we arrived on scene, however, there was no command center. *(It is important to note, that the original command center was in the lobby of South Tower prior to the collapse.)* There was no control, and it was every person or unit for themselves. We saw very little organization.

That is not a criticism; it was just reality.

After the South Tower collapsed at 9:58 a.m., there was no radio or cell communication in the area. The spire on top of World Trade Center's South Tower supported most of the communication network for much of the area, including New York City, parts of New Jersey, local aviation, and marine units.

All communication was down.

Additionally, there was no electric service south of Times Square. Teams were operating independently; it was organizational chaos on an unimaginable level, but that did not stop anyone from getting the job done. First responders in the New York and New Jersey area are some of the best trained in the world. While they faced insurmountable command and leadership challenges based on the communications failures during the 9/11 response, the responding teams and individuals were laser focused and instinctually fell in line to get the job done.

As an uninvited guest to a scene with no command or control, where we were there on a rogue, unauthorized mission, and quite frankly, in complete defiance of our agency, it was up to me to find purpose and determine how I could be most helpful, so I went back to my roots. I located the Office of Chief Medical Examiner's substation to meet with an old mentor of mine. To protect his identity, I will call him Sam.

I was directed to the area of The Atrium, a glass structure to the west of where the Twin Towers once stood. The once vibrant, glass-covered building filled with plant life and people communing over work conversation, talks of vacation plans, and stories of how one's kids did in local sports over the weekend was now a pile of shattered glass, broken dreams and the ever-present smell of death.

It was next to impossible to separate people's personal items, "important papers", clothing and human remains. There was no sign of life, just paper and ash. And it was impossible to determine what was left behind by those lucky enough to escape, the possessions that remained with those who died in place or what fell from the sky when the building came down. I did learn one very important lesson as I stood there in what was left of the Atrium that day. All the "things" we believe are so important, at some point or another, like all of the TPS reports and other meaningless paperwork, none of that mattered.

And to think, some associate might have gotten chewed out for a misspelling after submitting the report to a boss and someone else stressed about where to file it.

What folder?

What drawer?

How could anyone have known those reports would be discarded onto the streets of New York City like they never existed? Of all those who felt those papers were so important, I wonder … how many missed their kids' youth sports games for the sake of those "important papers?" How many calls from parents went straight to voicemail because they were too busy to talk? And how many times did these same people argue with a colleague over something so meaningless?

This was my first lesson on how to change my own way of living, the way I live now. The life lens I look through today is much clearer than it was back then. I've learned to give myself and others grace, especially when we make mistakes. And as for those mistakes, it is important to remember that we should grow and learn from them rather than resent them. The lesson here …

Do not sweat the little things.

Do them right, but don't sweat them.

I experienced a lifetime of emotions during my time at Ground Zero. One of my best friends from college, who was also my roommate and otherwise family to me, worked for a company headquartered in the South Tower. I knew he was at work that day, but it did not occur to me right away that he could have been lost in the collapse. Following the crash of the first plane, he ran and left everything behind. He had no wallet and no cell phone, and even if it did, the phone would not have worked anyway. He was disoriented and in shock. It wasn't until much later in the evening that anyone would hear from him, including his wife. He first had to get out of the City and find a place to make a call.

When he reached out to me later that night, I told him I was in the City doing whatever I could to help. I remember a long pause on the phone and then him begging me to get out of there. I told him that I wasn't going home until I had exhausted my ability to help.

"Well, if you are going to be there anyway," he replied. "Can you please look for my wallet? It was in my top desk drawer."

The dark humor was quite typical of my friend, and we both laughed. To this day, when we occasionally talk about 9/11, the running joke is that I was there trying to find his wallet, but I failed in my mission. I still reassure him, however, that I am not a quitter and one day I will find it. While our conversation is truly all in good fun, there is still a piece of me that wants to go back there, to that place and time, every time I say it. That comment, in jest or not, is symbolic of the guilt I feel for not having done more, for not having saved anyone, for not having completed the mission. That day, my college buddy's life obviously changed forever, too, but he always says for the better.

I envy that.

He has moved forward from that experience, taking with him the perspective to live every day like it's his last. He adds the caveat though, "Just do it responsibly, in case it's not." This is the truest definition of resilience. He did more than bounce back from a life-altering experience. He bounced forward. He allowed for an incredible level of post traumatic growth because he did not get stuck in a fixed mindset. He used the experience to make himself better.

John and I stayed well into the night to do what we could. We returned home later that evening to a place that looked the same but was now somehow different. Like many other communities, East Windsor was now changed forever. The town we worked in and where I grew up, lost three prominent residents. The town next to us, Cranbury, was the home of Todd Beamer. A few days after this catastrophic event, there were signs and flags posted in yards and storefronts that read, "Let's Roll!" Those were Todd's famous last words before trying to overtake the terrorists. There were sad and angry faces everywhere I turned, and a deafening silence on the streets and in every store.

I returned to Ground Zero for two more days on my own to help in the cleanup and recovery. I was on autopilot. Eventually, I had to get back to my regularly scheduled workdays—three on and three off. Truthfully, I still try my best to fill in the mental gaps of my time spent in lower Manhattan on those days, but the details are fuzzy, and it bothers me. I want to remember more. Time is also fuzzy, and it has only gotten fuzzier over the last 20+ years.

After the initial couple of days spent on scene, command and control began to take shape and the ICS and NIMS protocol started to fall in line. Five days in, the initial search and rescue morphed into a recovery and criminal investigation. The FBI took over and the human side of the mission began to fade. I went back a few times as a volunteer, but because I was not representing an agency that was part of the official mutual-aid paradigm, I was not able to help in any meaningful way. That was devastating to me.

Weeks and months went by, and my routine was back to normal. However, my heart and soul were on the Pile across the river. I never really talked about it to my family and friends. I certainly never talked about it to my peers at work because John and I went there against department orders. It was just a faded memory of something I did. I kept it in a locked box inside my head, but every now and then I would peek inside to make sure it was still there.

The week before Thanksgiving 2001, I got called into the lieutenant's office and was served an Internal Affairs complaint for policy violations regarding our "unauthorized efforts" at Ground Zero. It was a true blow to my spirit and passion for why I became a cop. I, (We), (Society), was confronted with the greatest assault on our country in its history, with the greatest loss of life on American soil *ever!*

I was a police officer, sworn to uphold the law, to protect and to serve, and to preserve life above all else. I was trained to do this work. We, as humans, have a responsibility to other humans to do good for them. I took the hit and did not dispute or appeal the charges. I felt if I had done so, I would look like a fool. Instead, I felt by accepting the charges, my administration would look like the fools. I ended up with a written reprimand, which was pled down from the initial recommendation of a three-day suspension. When word got around at the station, others struggled to believe it, and much of the rank-and-file lost respect for the brass.

Fools!

I did not return to the site to volunteer after that. Quite frankly, I was ordered not to, but I was still captivated by it all—the news reporting, people I knew who were still working the site and friends who ran right to the nearest recruiter's office to enlist in the United States military. I was feeling left behind, and I had a similar reaction to "survivor's guilt."

A lot would happen over the next year. I met Stephanie, the woman who would become my wife. My mom got sick and passed away; I was left to care for my grandmother, and life evolved into adulthood rather quickly. I was past the point of enlisting into the military, especially if I wanted to keep my wife and job, and, so, time marched forward. I never went back to the World Trade Center site, and I never dealt with my emotions surrounding it. I would only start talking about my experience years later when social media became a thing. Once a year, I would share my pictures as an obligatory memory of 9/11 with the expected caption, "Never Forget!"

CHAPTER TEN
Pandora's Box

I n September 2019, I began my terminal leave prior to my retirement which was set for the following December 31st. Eighteen years had passed since that harrowing day of the terrorist attacks, but to me it felt like it was yesterday. Time stood still for nearly two decades, and my soul never left the Pile. Additionally, I never went back to see the memorial or the museum. It wasn't because I did not want to. I did, but frankly, I did not want to open up Pandora's box and face my own emotions. In a weird way, I was afraid of closure because a part of me still wanted to go back and pick up where I left off, knowing damn well that would never be possible. I did not want to face the reality that life had moved on without me. I did not deal with my emotions back in September 2001, and I did not deal with them years later either. It was just easier to keep them packed away.

In early November 2019, my wife, Stephanie, had a meeting at Live Nation in Lower Manhattan, a block from the new 9/11 memorial. She encouraged me to go with her. I was upset with her for even suggesting it. I was dumbfounded that she could be so insensitive to push the issue. I recognized, however, how childish I was acting. So, like a good husband, I reluctantly agreed.

"Let's do this."

We took the train into the City together. The hour-long ride felt like 10, and yet when we got there, I was not ready to get off. We exited the New Jersey Transit train in Penn Station, then took a car that shuttled us downtown. I experienced a level of anxiety I had never felt before. It was different than when I rode the FDNY fireboat toward the billowing smoke of 9/11. It was different than forgetting my homework or getting called to the lieutenant's office for an Internal Affairs complaint. It was the anxiety of facing my emotions, dealing with something that was taking place deep inside of me. I felt so isolated and alone, no matter how many people were around me.

The car dropped my wife at her meeting, and then I continued on my own to the sacred site where I would reconnect with a lost part of me, reuniting with my soul. I was both sweaty and chilled. My heartbeat was fast and irregular, and my legs (especially my knees) felt weak. I slowly made my way to the memorial and museum. Consciously putting one foot in front of the other, I took deep, controlled breaths with each advancement of my left foot. I heard my academy drill instructor calling cadence in my head. Emotionally, walking back to that site was one of the hardest things I have ever done. I remember walking up to the main entrance. I was frozen, staring at the door. I heard a voice calling to me.

"Sir, can you help me? Sir, I'm over here!"

I was nauseous, and I felt helpless.

It was September 11, 2001, all over again.

As I turned toward the voice, I saw a woman looking at me through a glass window. She knocked on the pane to get my attention. I looked back with hopelessness in my eyes. I heard her voice again, only she wasn't asking for help. She was offering it.

"Sir, can I help you? Would you like a ticket to visit the museum? This is the window." I shook off the glazed stare and approached her. She clearly had seen that look before.

"Were you there that day," she asked.

"Yes," I replied, with some reservation. I presented her with my badge and police ID. Realizing I was a first responder, the woman handed me a complimentary ticket and directed me through the door.

It was early on a Tuesday morning, and I was the first visitor of the day. I was greeted by a staff member, a museum volunteer who said that she would be my companion during my visit. I laughed nervously and joked with her.

"Cool," I replied. "I promise not to tell my wife."

The elderly woman did not find my comment as funny as I did and, clearly, it was not the first time she had been confronted with cop humor. However, she gave me a warm and comforting introduction, sharing how she would be there for me if I needed anything, but she would not interact directly with me unless I initiated the conversation. The woman compared herself to an emotional support animal. I giggled to myself as she, in fact, reminded me of a 15-year-old poodle who was frail on the outside, but still had a loving heart and the desire to please.

I slowly made my way through the museum and read almost every exhibit marker. I cried a lot, but the support I received from my escort was second to none. I was doing well until I rounded a corner and came across the exhibit of the destroyed FDNY Ladder Company 3 fire truck.

I literally fell to my knees.

I could not understand why I got so emotional, but the panic, grief, and overwhelming sadness was real. I was assisted to my feet and walked to a nearby bench by my escort. I don't know why, but I began to scroll through pictures on my phone.

Then I saw it!

I had a photograph of that fire truck from the scene, where it rested in peril after being crushed by falling debris. An FDNY engine and all its equipment and crew that would never return. I showed the picture to my escort. She also became emotional. She called for the exhibit curator and asked me to share the photograph with him. I shared the image with the curator, and I learned that it was the first picture he had seen of that truck at the scene. I was able to share it with the museum, and it is now a part of the official record from that day. In that moment, I had a strong sense of closure.

Mission complete.

I share that with you because, as first responders, we never know how long it will take to get to that point of knowing or finding our purpose. When I look back to 9/11, I feel I did not fulfill all that I believe I could have or should have in terms of the rescue effort. However, 18 years later, I was able to give one more thing and get the gift of closure by sharing that picture. It is a small thing that will not change history, but for me it closed the circle.

To this day, I still get emotional when I talk about 9/11. I still get angry. I still feel hate. I cannot find forgiveness in my heart.

I don't think I ever will.

Over the course of the last 20+ years, the details from that day have become as fuzzy as my pictures. What still lives with me, as clear as if it were yesterday, are the smells, the tastes, and the sounds that are forever imprinted on my soul.

I am grateful to those who answered the call that day and the days, weeks, and years that followed. There are so many stories of true heroes who spent the rest of their career dedicated to the investigation, clean-up, and rebuilding. Many of whom have suffered physically and emotionally ever since. There are still 9/11 rescuers getting sick and dying from their service on the Pile or who succumb to the physical and emotional injuries they received.

I am equally as grateful for those who served our great nation and took the fight to the enemy. So many selfless men and women were driven to raise their right hand, place their left on the Bible, and swear an oath to protect this country from all enemies, foreign and domestic. They are the warriors of our time, men and women who we owe a debt of gratitude that can never be repaid in full.

They have all earned my highest respect.

To those who took that oath, I say, "You did your job, and you did it well. You were the sheepdogs who kept the wolf at bay. You were the ones who stopped evil from reaching our shores ever again. And you did it against all odds … with little support from feckless politicians who have the spines of an ameba.

You fought the foreign enemy with the business side of your M-14 and the domestic enemy with your battle-tested wisdom. In the end, it was bad policy that forfeited the objective, not *your* will or ability to succeed."

Reflecting on the botched Afghanistan withdrawal in August 2021, declaring all American involvement ended and turning the country back over to the terrorists, I want you all to remember that your service and sacrifice was worthwhile. We have had a policy and political setback, for sure, but I believe in my heart that it is only a setback.

You gave two generations of Afghans the tools they needed to get past this. Any failure is held in the hands of the President of the United States and his administration, not yours. You are all heroes!

Don't ever forget that.

◈

Following September 11th, I met the woman who would become my wife. I lost my mom and grandmother. I had three kids, several different homes, and a complete law enforcement career that ended with my scheduled retirement in January 2020. Throughout all my professional and personal achievements, I never talked about the *one* thing that shaped much of who I am—the events of 9/11. It was not until the 20th anniversary that I spoke publicly about my experience.

When I reflect on the emotional stress and trauma that I carried for so many years following that day, I realize that 9/11 is not what defines me. What defines me is 9/12.

Every year I attend some sort of 9/11 memorial service. It allows me to pay tribute to those lost on that day, especially those heroes who ran towards the danger to help those running away from it. I recall the stories of heroism, courage, and love of others, but most of all, I remember September 12, 2001. I recall how we were truly "one nation under God, indivisible, with liberty and justice for all."

I remember flags flying on every home, every business, every street corner, every car, and in every hand. I remember patches from police and fire departments around the country and around the world posted at the command center in Lower Manhattan. I remember seeing messages of hope, prayer, and compassion written anywhere there was space and spoken anyplace someone could be heard. I remember how we treated each other with respect because we saw one another as Americans, not an affiliate of a political party, race, religion, or gender identity. We were all just Americans.

Unhyphenated Americans!

I have always been a proud, flag-flying American. I bleed red, white, and blue, and I have since the day I was born. For those who know me, the flag is my logo and a part of my brand. However, on September 12, 2001, I had never felt prouder to be an American. I had never been more invested in serving her ideals and more committed to making every day, for the rest of my life, feel like 9/12. While I will *never forget* 9/11, I will always remember and celebrate 9/12.

Our country has been through a lot over the last 20+ years. We have fought the war on terror on many fronts. We have been fraught with divisive politicians, all claiming they would be "the one" to unite us. We have suffered many natural disasters and had media and special interest groups drive wedges through every community from sea to shining sea, all in an attempt to further their own individual agendas.

In 20 years, we have gone from the most unifying day in American history since July 4, 1776, to a culture of extreme divisiveness. We have perverted our values, lost our focus, and forgotten our purpose. And to those who believe we need to rewrite the Constitution of the United States, I challenge you to reread it first. It is the same Constitution that gives you the inalienable right to challenge it. If you have any integrity at all, you will reconsider your progressive push to "fundamentally change America."

So, this year and on every anniversary of the 9/11 Terror Attacks, I encourage you to pause, recall, honor, and speak the names of the 3,000 lives lost that day and the more than 3,000 lives that have been lost since. Take the time to show respect for the courage of those who answered the call as first responders and those who raised their right hand to serve the United States Armed Forces and take the fight to those who brought terror to our shores. And when the fanfare and memorials are over, I beg of you to remember September 12, 2001.

Find a way to be a proud American, "one nation under God, indivisible, with liberty and justice for all." For *that* is the legacy that best honors the memories of those who made the ultimate sacrifice.

22Zero

When I was asked to speak publicly for the 20th anniversary of 9/11, I was terrified. It wasn't because I was scared to speak in front of an audience. I had done that many times before. The truth is, I was scared of the emotional response to my own thoughts as I wrote the speech and my own words as they passed through my lips. Prior to my speech, my friend, John Walker, introduced me to the founder of 22Zero. This non-profit organization offers free services to veterans and first responders suffering from trauma and post-traumatic emotional responses.

I went through their "Trauma Resiliency-Protocol (TR-P) for PTSD and acute stress, as well as the Emotions Management Process (EMP) for negative emotions, like anger, anxiety, fear, sadness, and survivor's guilt, etc. At first, it felt like some voodoo shit or, as John described it, a Jedi-mind trick. However, at the conclusion of the process, I was exhausted and ready for a good nap. The feeling of wanting to sleep was noticeable to me because I don't sleep well, and I often fight the urge to sleep. When my brain relaxes, that's when all my thoughts turn to shit. The facilitator asked how I was feeling, and to be honest, I wasn't sure. I explained that I did not feel any different, but I *was* tired.

"Good," he replied. "That is exactly how you should feel."

He told me that after a few good nights of sleep, I would notice an emotional difference. I laughed and said, "It's been many years since I have had a few good nights of sleep. This might have been a waste of your time."

The facilitator assured me I would be fine, and sure as shit, I had never slept better than I did the next few nights. As a result, my days were brighter, and I felt more refreshed. I was no longer snapping at my family in anger, and I wrote my speech without any hesitation. On top of which, I presented it without a moment of any emotional angst.

What the fuck just happened?

Who am I and where did the miserable version of myself go?

While I loved how I was transforming, there was a small part of me that missed the asshole I once was, but I certainly will never miss the anxiety and sleepless nights. There was a bit of my identity, a battle scar, that went along with being a train wreck that I was going to miss, too. However, this new and improved me was pretty cool.

TR-P and EMP holds their root in neuro-linguistic programming and are clinically researched and approved. While there is no magic for healing post-traumatic stress, this process comes pretty damn close.

Thank you, Dan Jarvis, for all your work and for giving me my sanity back. Johnny, I love ya, brother! Thank you for guiding me towards Dan and 22Zero. For the rest of you suffering in silence, please visit www.22zero.org and watch "Healing the Heroes of 9/11—The Way Forward." It is an incredible documentary directed and produced by Michael Gier, someone I can also now call a friend. The film features the 22Zero program. And yes, my good friend and brother, Johnny, is in the movie!

CHAPTER ELEVEN
Family First, Always

F amily is our history, our foundation, our support, and our motivation. It is who we are at our core—for better or for worse. It is how we are often defined by others. No matter who we are or where we come from, the importance of family cannot be understated. That goes across the board, no matter your economics, race, religion, nationality, etc. Those family relationships can be represented by the "normal" nuclear family, professional family, friends that feel like family, youth sports teams, religious family, first responder family, military family, criminal gangs, and any other groups of individuals with a common purpose and identity.

As police officers, we are taught that we represent two families when working the streets—the name on the patch affixed to our shoulder and the name on the plate affixed to our chest. We are reminded to never dishonor either.

Your family is your brand.

For those who binge-watch television, think *Yellowstone*. Throughout my life, I have personally identified with many different kinds of families. Each has had a hand in shaping who I am. The people within these different "families" have played important roles, whether it was short term or long term. The impact and time frame are not necessarily connected. Throughout my life, my nuclear family has ***always*** been at the core of who I am as David Berez—husband, dad, and man.

When talking about my biological family, it is important to go back in history and talk about where I came from, where my family came from. I am of German descent on my mother's side and of Ukrainian/Russian descent on my father's side. As a result of the family relationships during my childhood, I am much more familiar with the history on my mother's side, but thanks to working with my cousins on my father's side, I continue to learn more about my Ukrainian/Russian roots all the time.

My German Roots

My grandfather, Helmut Wolff, whom I called Opa (German for grandpa) was born to Heinrich and Selma Wolff in Nackenheim, Germany in 1915. Nackenhein sits along the Rhein River, the heart of German wine country near the city of Mainz. My grandfather's family was involved with farming and supported the community through local industry and tourism. They were a well-respected, upper-middle-class family.

Both of my grandparents were raised in Jewish families, and while neither was especially religious, both families were steeped in tradition of Jewish values, customs, and identity. Both the Wolff and Scheuer (my grandmother's side) families were significant contributors to their individual communities and well respected by neighbors, businesses, client partners, and local political leadership. Sadly, that all came crashing down with little notice.

It was early October 1938 when the weight of the Nazi Party in Germany came bearing down on "non-believers." While those living this transition in real time saw the change as sudden, history has shown us otherwise. Hitler's rise to power was a long time coming and was in the works for nearly half a generation. Rights of independence were slowly eroded and replaced with rights of the government, imposing their views on people, telling them what to think and believe. Of the many eroding rights were the infringement of free speech, free press, and gun ownership. One of the antisemitic ideologies being used to brainwash the Germans was that the Jewish people were a significant cause of all that ailed Germany. My great grandparents, Heinrich and Selma, were smart, educated people, not to mention selfless parents. They planned for their sons, Helmut and Herbert, to sail to America to live with distant cousins, safe from the Nazi rule and persecution. The plan was for Selma and Heinrich to ride out the "storm," protect the family business, and eventually bring their sons back to Germany when the political tension eased.

Helmut entered the United States through Ellis Island, beginning his new life in a new land at the age of 21. Herbert remained in Germany to attend medical school but was forced out after his freshman year for being Jewish. He soon followed Helmut to New York.

My grandfather and his parents exchanged many letters over the next several weeks and months. Heinrich wrote how life was getting much harder in Germany and their freedoms were limited to none. He told how he and Selma were secretly being brought food and water in the middle of the night by the Sands family, risking their own lives for supporting a Jewish family. The Sands Family also helped my great-grandparents bury their gold and other treasures, so it would be safe until after the fall of the Nazi Party.

In their final letter to Helmut, Selma and Heinrich shared how they would soon be collected by the Nazis and taken to a work camp. The camp was called Dachau. They were to be held there, used in service to the

Nazis' and then returned to society once they had been "re-educated." They noted that there were other Jewish families who had already been relocated to camps, but they had no further communication with them. This letter, which hangs on my office wall to this day, was the last communication my grandfather had from his parents. Selma and Heinrich were never heard from again. My family later learned that they were both exterminated in the Dachau Concentration Camp.

While Helmut and Herbert lived with both the guilt and gratefulness for their new American life over the next 60 years, they showed incredible resilience. In light of losing their parents, they discovered new family members in the New York area, along with work that would support them and their goals.

My grandfather taught me what it meant to be a patriot and to believe in America. I will always remember when he told stories about seeing the Statue of Liberty when the ship entered New York harbor and, in that moment, he knew everything was going to be okay.

He recalled when the ship docked and what it felt like to step onto American soil for the first time. He looked up towards God to express his gratitude, and his nearsighted vision was filled with the American Flag. He never considered himself a German from that moment forward, and for the rest of his life, he would raise and lower the American Flag every morning and every night. He knew he was now an American, and he was going to work every day to honor that privilege.

When he died in 1998, one of this nation's most grateful patriots died, too. My grandfather, Helmut Wolff, taught me what it means to appreciate being an American, and I hope that I have lived up to his expectations.

❧

As I mentioned earlier, my mother's side of the family is all from Germany. I am only the second generation to be born here in the United States from her side, my mom being the first. My grandmother was born Elfrieda Scheuer in 1921 to Rosa (Borg) and Emil Scheuer in Staudernheim, Germany. Staudernheim is a small town along the Nah River in central Germany. At the time, it was a nondescript, quintessential European town from the early 1900s, filled with middle-class residents who were well-educated and lived an otherwise good, prosperous, and love-filled life. The community was a mixture of Jews and Christians working and living together. These individual identities were celebrated, rather than despised.

In the middle of October 1938, the Nazi Party was nearing full control of Germany and gaining power in other parts of Europe. I recall stories that my grandmother told me about how she was isolated in school. She shared how her best friends would no longer play with her and how she would stand under a specific tree in the school yard because that is where she felt safe. My grandmother and her family, also German Jews, recognized that their lives were in jeopardy and the entire family made arrangements to leave Germany for the United States. The Scheuer family (Emile, Rosa, Elfrieda and Edith) each had a ticket to board the USS Washington in the middle of November, departing Hamburg, Germany, bound for the New York harbor.

My grandmother, who had just turned 17 years old, packed all she could into a single suitcase. The family heirlooms were packed in a large trunk regularly used for overseas travel. Like the last letter from my great-grandparents, I still have that travel trunk with all of the original shipping stickers affixed to it. I use it as a couch table in my home.

By the first week in November, their bags were packed, and the Scheuer family was making final preparations to travel to the United States of America. Then on November 9th, life and hope would change course. Nazi leaders unleashed a series of pogroms against the Jewish population in Germany and recently incorporated territories. These violent riots were incited with the aim of massacring or expelling an entire religious group. This event came to be called Kristallnacht (The Night of Broken Glass) because of the shattered glass that littered the streets after the vandalism and destruction of Jewish-owned businesses, synagogues, and homes. This destruction included a family-owned hotel in Sankt Goarshausen across from the Lorelei. This hotel was later repaired by the Nazis and used as their regional headquarters.

I should note, Sankt Goarshausen and the Lorelei remain of great interest to tourists to this day, and the hotel still exists. The hotel was owned by my grandmother's family. My grandfather's family sold wine and other consumables to the hotel. My grandparents were just kids at the time, and I don't believe they knew each other, even though the extended families did. We would later learn that my grandparents were cousins by marriage, and that relationship was formed from the business relationship. As I mentioned earlier, family is formed in many different ways and the same people can often overlap.

Bet you didn't see that coming.

Days after Kristallnacht, my grandmother's family received a telegram from family in the United States. Due to safety concerns, the USS Washington would not be porting in Hamburg, and its last port of call before returning to the United States would be in Le Havre, France. Suddenly, the Scheuer family needed to find a way out of Germany in order to quickly get to Le Havre. So, with cash on hand and whatever they could carry, the family set off for France. They left everyone and everything behind. While they did not know it at the time, and it was certainly not their intent, the Scheuers would never return to Germany.

Upon their arrival in Le Havre, they found the ship already in port and crowds of unticketed passengers trying to board, in hopes of escaping the German borders and getting to America. They, too, had learned of the ship's itinerary change. Fortunately, the Scheuers had boarding passes and were able to take refuge on the USS Washington toward freedom.

After weeks of travel, my grandmother and her family arrived at Ellis Island. They were processed in the exact same way you likely learned about in school or have seen in a movie. They eventually settled in a Lower East Side apartment in Manhattan after a short stay in St. Louis, Missouri with other family and began to make a new life for themselves. They, too, were the definition of resilient. My grandmother finished her schooling, her parents found meaningful work, and they quickly earned their US Citizenship.

∽

I cannot remember if this story is attributed to my grandmother or grandfather, but it is too good not to tell. One of them had started selling pencils in New York City. It was a pencil-pyramid scheme. They were given one pencil to sell and instructed to bring the money back to the boss afterward.

Mission complete.

Then they were given two pencils. If both pencils sold, they were able to keep the earnings from one pencil and return the earnings for the second. Then there were four pencils, then eight and so on. This was the entrepreneurial and survival spirit that laid the foundation for my family for generations to come.

While my grandmother's family left the City first, settling in the small town of South River, New Jersey, my grandmother traveled back to Manhattan often until she would eventually move there at the age of 23. It is interesting to note that South River's immigrant community was largely made up of Germans, Poles, and Russians. It was later discovered that many were Nazi defectors, as the party began to fall and implode. My grandmother's next-door neighbor was ultimately found to be a high-ranking Nazi official connected to Josef Mengele. Mengele was an officer and physician known as the Angel of Death to his victims.

My grandparents, Helmut and Elfrieda, met through their German-Jewish communities and eventually fell in love. They made the connection regarding their families in Germany, recognizing that *they* were already a family and marriage was just a formality. While they initially lived together in Manhattan, they left New York City for the suburbs of New Jersey and settled about 30 miles southwest in a small, undeveloped town called East Brunswick, just south of South River. They bought a small chicken farm that averaged 3,000 birds and sold the eggs locally—door to door. As the business and community grew, my grandparents thrived.

They were members of a prominent synagogue in the city of New Brunswick where they met other Jewish families who had settled in the area. One of those families was the Kaufelts, German farmers who had a small farmstand on the main road connecting New Brunswick to growing resort communities near the New Jersey beaches. My grandparents supplied this small market with eggs, and the first business-to-business relationship was born. Mr. Kaufelt grew his small farmstand to a larger market, a brick-and-mortar store known as Kaufelt's. It was the first known supermarket and later became the corporate entity, Foodtown. My grandparents were the primary egg supplier of the East Brunswick store for many years.

My grandfather was always looking to better himself, grow his financial worth, and provide a good life for his family. While he was a good man and well intentioned, he was not great at expressing love and was not perceived as a great husband or father. I can say, though, he was a great grandfather whom I loved dearly. I learned so much from him in the 23 years we shared on this earth together. He was a great businessman in his early years and grew to own shares in several properties throughout the New Brunswick area. He earned his realtors license, was a tool-and-die maker and, of course, a farmer.

My grandfather did have one financial failure though. He was offered to buy a 10-acre piece of property along the dirt road where Mr. Kaufelt had his market. It was 10 acres for the price of $3,000. My grandfather did not see value in a sandy lot along a dirt road to nowhere.

Why was this a financial failure?

That dirt road is now New Jersey Route 18 in East Brunswick, New Jersey and the sandy lot was ultimately developed into one of *the* largest shopping malls in the state. The man who bought that property sold it for $100 million to the developer. I often think how different my life would have been if he made that purchase. Looking back, I am glad he didn't buy it. I like my life. I can't imagine it being any different.

My grandfather was a true American Patriot and, like I said before, he was a great influence on my life. He taught me how to be a gentleman. He taught me how to be accountable. He taught me how important it is to provide for my family. The most important thing I learned from him, however, was how to respect the opportunities I have as an American. I learned to love the one tangible item he loved the most—the American flag. The symbolism of that flag to him represented freedom, opportunity, and home. Every morning he raised the flag and then every night he lowered it. If he was away from the house for any reason, the first thing he would do when he returned home was post the colors. I will never forget when he returned home from the hospital after his first heart attack in 1988. Before going inside, he insisted on posting the flag.

"I need to put up my flag to let everyone know I am home, and I am alive," he exclaimed.

That flag was a part of his brand, and it is a part of my brand, too. The flag is my calling card, just like it was his. I cannot fully articulate everything it means to me.

One of the many things I admire most about my grandfather is that he loved to network and get to know everyone who crossed his path. He was never looking for new friends or looking to take advantage of his connections. He truly wanted to be there for anyone who ever needed anything. He had so many great people in his life who relied on him for his generosity and so many people he could call on if he ever needed anything. And if he could not personally help, his consistent response was, "I know a guy."

That was 100 percent true.

As close as my grandfather was with his circle of friends, he could never remember anyone's name. He always referred to people by something notable that uniquely represented them. For example, there was Pollock Joe (the plumber and carpenter), the Chinaman (another tool-and-die maker), the Shyster (the car salesman), Dirty Mike (the mechanic), and so on.

My grandfather was a shining light in my life and, if nothing else, we had one thing in common: we were the only two males on that side of the nuclear family and my mother and grandmother saw men as useful idiots. We knew our place in the rank structure of our family, and we related well to each other. For example, when others were surprised that I actually graduated high school and got into (and graduated) college, he was the one person who was genuinely proud of me. He was even prouder still when I was hired by the Seaside Park Police Department as a Class I Special Police Officer in May of 1998.

I saw him and my grandmother a few days before I went into the police academy. We were celebrating my sister's birthday. I told him I was to start the Class I Police Academy on June 3rd, and he started to cry.

"You are going to be the best police officer because you care about people, and you have empathy for those who are suffering. Someday you are going to be the chief, and you will be a great leader!" Then in German, with his hand on my face, he said, "Geh mit Gott. Ich liebe dich."

Go with God. I love you.

I started to cry, as my heart felt full and empty at the same time. I was 23 years old, and not only had he never said he loved me before, but I had also never heard him say it to anyone—ever. I believe in my heart he knew he was dying, but my brain did not allow me to even think it.

My Opa died on June 2, 1998, just two days later.

I started the Class I Academy the next day with a heavy heart, but I knew that my grandfather was smiling down on me. His pride in my endeavors will carry me through the rest of my days. My only regret is that he never saw me in uniform. It was the one thing I believe he was holding out for but did not get to see.

CHAPTER TWELVE
The Matriarchs

Growing up, I knew my grandmother as Ge. When she first became a grandmother, after my sister was born, Ge wanted to be called Grammie. However, when my sister, Rachel, first began to speak, the word "Grammie" came out as "Ge."

The name stuck.

Ge was a regular figure in my life. We saw her every weekend and often during the week. She lived 20 minutes away and would come to our house to support my mom in raising us. Ge was an amazing cook and baker; the food she made are some of my fondest memories of her.

Long before I was born, and while my mom was still in school, Ge was a baker in the elementary school in East Brunswick. If something was made with flour, sugar, eggs, and butter, Ge made the best version of it.

No exaggeration.

From pancakes to pretzels, donuts to croissants, and cookies to her famous cinnamon bread, she could bake the hell out of anything. She created the best holiday meals with matzo ball soup, brisket, and the best cooked carrots I have ever had. If you have ever experienced a traditional Jewish holiday meal, imagine adding a bit of German tradition and a shit ton of salt, sugar, and butter. And there you have it, the best meal—ever!

As you read in chapter four, my father was a complete fucking turd. He was never around to be a dad. My mom worked at several different jobs while I was growing up, and until my sister and I were old enough to care for ourselves, Ge was always there to pick up the pieces.

She was like a third parent to us. We often vacationed together and during the summer months, we spent weeks at a time at my grandparents' house.

Growing up, my relationship with Ge was great, but it was not until later in life that I realized how important it actually was. She was there for me my entire life and would support me in so many different ways. Ge made sure I was bilingual. She would speak to me as much in German as she would in English. She bought me my first car, and she paid my college tuition in cash, so that I could have a fresh start in life. More importantly, she gave the gift of everlasting love to all three of my children, one of which she did not live long enough to meet. She was an incredible knitter and made baby blankets for all her great grandchildren, who still use them to this day. Those blankets are referred to as Ge blankets in our house, and we all have one. I have so much more to share about Ge in her later years, but I want to introduce you to my mother first.

My mom, Linda Helen Wolff-Berez was, by all accounts, a great woman with a good heart and a warm soul. She saw her most important job in the world as being the best mother she could be. My mom was raised as a farm girl. She did not move to a conventional home in a suburban neighborhood until she was a pre-teen. She was an average student, a bit introverted, and a great daughter and granddaughter. My mom was the best sister she could be to her brother, but he was a weirdo from day one with an eccentric and flamboyant personality. He hated everything American and was incredibly difficult to get along with. To spite my grandparents, my uncle left New Jersey at the age of 24, following his formal studies, to live in Germany and to escape the Vietnam draft. He could have gone anywhere, but he chose Germany.

When my mom graduated high school, she went on to finishing and secretarial school to learn the ins and outs of being a secretary. Today she would be appropriately labeled an administrative or executive assistant. Towards the end of 1968, my mom and Ge headed to Israel where she met a nice woman named Wendy who lived in Yardley, Pennsylvania, not far from her. Wendy was the same age as my mom, and they stayed in touch following the trip. On New Year's Eve of that same year, Wendy invited my mom to her house for a party. The New Year's celebration was designed to introduce my mom to a man named Fred, a single friend of Wendy's fiancé Mike.

The two hit it off!

Fred was a smooth talker, an accountant by trade and a U.S. Army reservist on the weekends. For their first date, Fred picked my mom up at my grandparents' house, where she still lived. He was just returning from being a "weekend warrior" and was wearing his Army dress uniform. He drove a gold Buick Regal and had all the markings of her knight in shining armor. Fred was invited into the house and my grandfather, the patriot that he was, seemed as impressed with Fred as my mom was, maybe even more.

My parents were married in 1970, and my sister was born in 1971. I came along in 1975, and my mom's heart was full. She did not work outside the home for the first part of my life and was the best, most dedicated mother I could have ever wished for. I was a pretty sick kid in my earliest days, and mom spent a good part of her time staying home with me, taking me to doctor appointments and putting out "fires" at school as I got older.

I recall my mom and Ge telling stories of my first few weeks of life and how they were never sure of my survivability. They regularly talked about the time when I was only a few weeks old, and I had been taking an irregularly long nap. Ge shared how she walked into my bedroom to check on me in my crib and was horrified by what she found. I was face down, not breathing, and cyanotic.

I had turned blue.

Ge told how she quickly grabbed me up, shook me, and banged on my back to revive me. I always joked with her about it.

"That explains why I am such an idiot today! I was deprived of oxygen and suffered from shaken baby syndrome."

Just kidding, Ge!

Truth is, I am forever indebted to her for finding me and instinctively saving my life. She was not trained in any particular medical technique and had no experience in resuscitation. That was the first of hundreds of sinus infections I would have throughout my life.

Between birth and age seven, I had regular respiratory infections from sinus to tonsils to lungs. I missed as much school as I attended, and then during the summer of 1982, I had my tonsils and adenoids removed. It literally saved my life and allowed my body to slowly recover once the infections stopped. My mom went back to work as an administrative assistant once my health improved. She landed a position at Princeton University in the physics department and then the geo-sciences department. They were amazing opportunities for her, allowing her to thrive in a professional environment. The benefits she received helped absorb the college costs for both me and my sister. My mom remained with the university for almost 15 years.

The summer after I turned eight years old, my mom sent me to sleep-away camp for four weeks and then each summer that followed for the next eight years. I attended one of the Reform Jewish Camps called Camp Harlem. She felt that it would be a great opportunity for me to escape the tumultuous environment in my house, learn independence, find my own identity and grow in a way that was supported by our Jewish values. I was reluctant at first, but camp was the best thing that ever happened to me. To this date, one of my closest friends was a bunkmate, turned college roommate. I also remain connected to so many other friends I met through the camp experience.

While sleep away camp was originally a "Jewish" experience in the Northeast, it has become a growing experience for all our nation's youth. For those not familiar, sleep-away camp has its roots in Jewish immigration. In the late 1800's and early 1900's, Jewish immigrants would be off for the summer when the garment and other New York labor industries would shut down. The families would vacation together in mountain resorts in the Poconos and Catskills. As the industrial revolution rapidly grew, the men would remain in the City for the summer to work while the women and children occupied the resorts.

Then, as the economic depression affected income, women entered the workforce and sent their children alone to the summer programs. This was the birth of summer camp. One hundred years later, these camps are still thriving with a diversity of kids who learn to make relationships, enhance skills in areas of interest, like sports and art. And they get to try new things in a safe and nurturing environment. My kids now spend their summers doing the same.

*Thank you, Camp Greylock and Camp Romaca for being a part of **my** children's journey.*

My years as a volunteer EMT took me out of the house much more than my mom would have liked. My experiences as a first responder stole my innocence, something she worked so hard to protect.

I think that broke her heart.

My college years gave me the independence my mom always pushed for, but it also pulled her baby from her arms. It was a challenging paradox for her. As I began adulthood, taking on my forever job as a police officer and moving into my first home made her feel alone, as if her job was done. All my mom ever wanted was to be a mom. Time flew by faster than she anticipated, and before she knew it, she was living in a five-bedroom home on a half-acre lot all by herself.

My relationship with my mom had its challenges when I became an adult, and as I got older, I shamefully became less appreciative of all she had done for me. However, she never regretted or resented it. She just continued to be my mom. While I grew to learn and appreciate all that my mom had done to protect me and provide opportunities for me to grow, I did not always show my appreciation. Today, I know my mom did her best to support and nurture me, and I wish she was here so that I could show her my appreciation in real time.

When I told her that I wanted to be a police officer, everything changed. She was not supportive, and for some reason, she felt betrayed. We fought regularly, and our relationship was strained. I was hired by the East Windsor Police Department at the same time my sister got married and planned to move several hours away. I made a deal with my sister that I would rent her townhouse from her in a nearby community until I was able to buy it.

So, as we helped my sister pack up her place, I don't think the truck had even crossed the state line before I started to move my stuff in. I was so excited to have my own home and start adulting.

My mom, on the other hand, took it personally.

She viewed my wanting to get out of her house as a sign of disrespect. She was right, but at the same time she was wrong. I wanted out because I wanted to grow, just like she pushed me to do my entire life. She wanted me to stay because she was scared that we were all leaving her behind.

I get it now.

I just wish I would have seen it then.

I would have been more sympathetic. I would have shown more gratitude, and I would have probably even said, "I love you."

When it comes to my mom, there are a lot of things I *should have* done, things I now regret. So, I urge you … if your parents are still alive, love them now. As my buddy Tim likes to say, "Don't "shoulda" all over yourself."

I should note that when I took my first resiliency class in 2020, I wrote a gratitude letter to my mom. (That is where I got the idea, which I include in chapter four.) While I could not call her up and read it to her over the phone or drop it in the mail, I did read it at her grave site, and I left it there for her. I hope it helps her soul rest in peace, as it was certainly a cathartic exercise for me.

My relationship with my mom was a challenge, and after I moved, she did not talk to me for almost a full year. Mom never showed up to my house and would not interact with me when I showed up at hers. She never came to a place of acceptance that I was a grown-ass man. It makes me sad because I am the person I am today because of her, not in spite of her, and she could not see that. I have become a community caretaker, a child advocate, an empathetic police officer, a dedicated husband, and a good father because of all that she taught me. She could not see any of that because she resented my independence. The same independence she worked so hard to teach me.

But she was dug-in.

The tension between my mother and me eased over time, but our relationship was never the same after I moved out. It wasn't until after my experiences on 9/11 that we both took stock of our lives. We each realized that our time here on Earth is short, and that we ought to make the best of it. As we were rebuilding, my mom was hopeful I would find the woman of my dreams. While I certainly found many women that dreams are made of, it took some time to find the one who would complete me. I had several practice relationships and one dress rehearsal, but it was not until June 2002 that I found my leading lady.

CHAPTER THIRTEEN
Love & Loss

I met my wife, Stephanie, at a wedding in 2002. I was 27 years old, and I was scared to fall in love and to lose my independence that I had grown to enjoy. I could not comprehend sharing my life with someone when, frankly, I do not like sharing anything. The trouble is, I was smitten. Stephanie is not a fixer, enabler, or even all that empathetic. However, she is honest and tough, always forcing me to find the resilience needed to move forward. She is good at reminding me of my wins—the win, itself, and the "What's Important Now" (WIN), a compelling acronym derived from the famous Notre Dame football coach Lou Holtz. She is also quick to remind me of my impact on the world, especially when I am feeling down on myself.

Stephanie pushes me beyond my comfort zone, and I am always better for it. When we were dating, I knew where we were headed. I also knew that it was important that "this one" meet my mom. Over time, my mom and Stephanie formed a relationship, but I am not sure if my mom knew my intentions with "this one." I think she was afraid to lose me again, and that prevented her from getting too close.

In October 2003, my family got together for Rosh Hashana dinner at my mom's house. Ge was cooking, no surprise, and my sister, Rachel, her husband, and my three-year-old niece were playing in the living room. My mom was outside walking my dog, a sweet, smart, and stubborn German shepherd/chow mix with whom she had a love-hate relationship. Stephanie was with her family on Long Island for the holiday.

I was being my typical self, sitting back and watching it all as if it was a movie. I was only three years into being a police officer, but looking back, I was already struggling with my mental health. I was already displaying typical signs often seen in first responders, like being withdrawn from family and self-isolating. Even at that early stage, I felt like an outsider looking in. Whether it was family gatherings, parties, or a big event, I no longer felt connected to the people in the room or in the moment.

I felt far away.

This time was a bit different though. I was missing Stephanie. As I watched my sister and her family, I contemplated having my own family someday. I was imagining Stephanie's mothering skills, and what holidays might look like as our families grew up together. Then, in an instant, everything in my life changed. I was suddenly humbled by the realization that sometimes when men make plans, God laughs.

However, this was not funny, and I was not laughing.

My mom came into the house through the garage. She was not holding onto the dog's leash, and she seemed upset and confused. My dog darted in behind her and also appeared quite anxious and jumpy, taking quick, short, stutter steps in a way I had never seen before. My mom sat down and began to cry.

"I couldn't pick it up. I couldn't do it," she whimpered. "I tried to pick up the dog's poop, but I couldn't do it."

"I'll do it," I said, assuring her it was no problem. After all, it was my dog. As I stepped outside, I could not help but think that this was yet another unbelievable overreaction on her part, but then again, it was my mom. Every time something went wrong, and it had anything to do with me, I got the blame.

I could not do anything right.

When I came back inside, everyone was in my mom's bedroom, and she was lying in bed. She had calmed down a bit and explained that she was not able to pick up the poop because it was not where her eyes saw it. Every time she bent down, her hand was six inches from where it needed to be, and it would not go to the place her brain was telling it. As she spoke, her speech began to slur, the right side of her face began to droop, and her right arm went numb.

With my background as a first responder and my sister being a nurse, we saw all the signs. We believed our mom was having a stroke, so we called EMS. For those who have never been a first responder and don't know how the backend of a 9-1-1 call works, here is what goes on: I dialed the number, and the local dispatcher answered.

"9-1-1, what's your emergency?"

Recognizing the voice, I replied, "Hey, Veronica! It's David Berez. I'm at my mom's house, and I think she is having a stroke."

In a calm voice, Veronica instructed, "Okay, bud. Stay on the line with me while I dispatch EMS and patrol."

I can't imagine Veronica would have called anyone else, "bud," but she was a longtime friend, colleague, and the best damn dispatcher I ever worked with. She treated us all like we were one of her own kids. After dispatching EMS, Veronica asked the usual questions.

What is your mom's name, address, and date of birth?

What is her medical history?

What are her symptoms?

Is she breathing, conscious, talking?

All the answers were transmitted to the responding units, so they would have an idea and visual of what they were walking into. When the cavalry arrived, the EMTs were volunteers I had trained. The paramedics were the ones who had trained me, and the police officers were brothers I went to work with every day. Everyone knew my mom's address, and everyone knew my family was the one in need. They also knew that I was the caller, and that if I had dialed 9-1-1 from my own home, in the town where I volunteered as an EMT and worked as a police officer, then I could not handle this on my own, and shit was bad, so EVERYONE CAME!!

Because family first, always!!

After a complete evaluation, the medics advised there were no clinical signs of anything medically wrong. Her EKG was normal, as was her pulse and breathing.

Are you fucking kidding me?

Was she looking for a pity party on a holiday because of my dog?

What the fuck?!

I began to lose my cool and was quickly taken out of the bedroom by one of the responding officers and one of the medics. While the officer did his best to calm me down and bring me back to center, the medic laid down a reality check.

"I know we are not seeing any clinical signs, but there is something wrong with your mom," he said. "She needs to go to the ER, and we should not be wasting time. I am concerned."

I trusted this guy with my life, literally. He saved my ass on a call years earlier. Therefore, I trusted him with my mom's life, too.

So, off to the hospital we went.

My mom spent two days at Robert Wood Johnson University Hospital in Hamilton, New Jersey. She underwent every possible test you can imagine. Her symptoms would come and go, but they mostly only subsided. A CT scan of her head showed a small bleed. I never did see the images, but that is what we were told. It seemed she had had a mild stroke and would be sent home with a recommendation to follow up with a cardiologist and neurologist.

Late on the second day, my mom was being discharged. She was literally being pushed out of the hospital in a wheelchair when the resident who had been tending to her and coordinating her care came running down the hall, calling out her name, "Ms. Berez, Ms. Berez!"

I thought we had forgotten something in the room.

He was holding a set of imaging films in his hand. Short of breath, he said, "We need to talk. There is something I need to tell you. You can't go home yet."

As a police officer and volunteer EMT, I have had many occasions where I needed to deliver bad news.

I knew that tone.

I knew his words.

I knew his angst.

I knew what was coming.

The doctor explained that he had just spoken with the neurologist, and they were no longer concerned about a stroke.

Damn. That's awesome!!

But wait; why was this guy all tangled up?

Then, he said it, "We believe she has an invasive brain tumor."

After hearing those words, I was overcome by the loudest silence that followed, the pause in the doctor's words as the rest of us were trying to process what he had just said. My mom was wheeled back upstairs for another day of testing, including a brain biopsy. She was released again the next day.

In the following days we met with renowned oncologist, Dr.

Michael J. Nissenblatt, and one of our nation's leading brain surgeons, Dr. Michael Nosko. We learned that my mom had a stage four astrocytoma, also known as a glioblastoma. These tumors are not curable, and they are a death sentence. However, they can be treatable to slow the growth. Many of you may recall this type of tumor found in John McCain, Ted Kennedy, Tug McGraw, and so many others. While only 15,000 new cases are discovered in the U.S. each year, approximately 0.0045% of the population, it seems like so much more. My mom's disease lasted eight-and-a-half weeks. It was short enough that her suffering was limited, but long enough that we were able to repair years of damage to our mother-son relationship.

We were able to part with love.

During the eight weeks, my mom and I endured a lot. My mom had major brain surgery that left her paralyzed on the right side. She tried really hard with her rehabilitation, and to this day, I cannot thank those at JFK Rehabilitation Hospital in New Jersey enough for all they did for her. Their compassion and motivation were infectious and truly gave us all hope, even though we knew the odds were against us. I learned how to care for my mom during this time, in a way that she would have cared for me. And I had eight weeks to learn how to be a parentless adult, like learning how to steer a rudderless ship during an ocean storm.

While I had emotional support from Stephanie, I was still managing it all on my own. My sister was back in Charlottesville, Virginia where she was waiting on the birth of her second child. My grandmother, Ge, was sitting idly by her dying daughter, wondering how she would move forward after burying her child.

Me? I was just me, operating in crisis-management mode, suppressing my emotions, getting shit done.

I was all business.

In the days leading up to my mom's death, my sister had a beautiful baby boy and was able to get to New Jersey in time, so my mom could hold her grandson. It was one of the most memorable moments of my life, a juxtaposition between life and death.

When one comes, one must go.

I was so happy for my sister, my mom, and my new nephew. In her dying moments, my mom would know that her daughter was married with two beautiful children and living a happy life. She would die with that image in her mind. It is everything that a parent could ask for.

But what about me?

How would she see me while taking her last breath?

✎

On November 29, 2003, I had not eaten anything of substance in some time. My mom was no longer conscious, and she had not communicated in a few days. All I could think about was that she was going to die without having any idea how my story would turn out. Stephanie and I had been together for 17 months, and my mom had gotten to know her well. She knew Stephanie's character and had learned to love her. She also met her parents who were both so supportive throughout this process.

I knew Stephanie was "the one" and an engagement and marriage was only a matter of time. So, with my mom's engagement ring in my possession, I paced through the house. I ate like a ravenous recruit the day after academy graduation, and I built up the courage to ask the question.

Stephanie knew something was up. She noticed my wolfish eating pattern, saw my angst, and was dialed into my sudden change in behavior. She has always been, and still is to this day, tuned into me. She notices the signs long before I see them in myself. We were sitting on the green couch in the living room, a fixture in our life. It was a hand-me-down, but it was ours and the only comfy place to sit in our house.

Everything happened on that couch.

Stephanie and I talked about the anticipated days ahead, and I expressed my sadness that my mom would never know my story. I added that she needed to know as much as possible, and then right there, in the midst of all that was going on, I got down on one knee, and in the presence of my dog ... (Yes, dog! Not God), I asked Stephanie to marry me.

While the proposal was not on some mountaintop with a blue-sky background or at sunrise on a lake, it was "our moment" and neither one of us will ever forget it. Over the next 24 hours, we told our family and friends, arranging for as many of them to be present at my mom's bedside when we told her the news. We also had our Rabbi present to perform a special blessing given to the families of the future bride and groom before the wedding. While this is customarily done the night before the wedding, time was not on our side. So, surrounded by our closest family and friends, the Rabbi gave the blessing at my mom's bedside.

For the first time in days, she smiled slightly from the left side of her mouth, and tears rolled out of her tightly closed eyes. I believe my mom thought Stephanie and I got married right there in front of her on that day. Whatever she was thinking, she knew who I would be spending the rest of my life with, and that gives me peace. However, what will continue to hurt for all the days of my life and be the hardest part for me to live with is that my mom never got to meet my children, and they never got to meet her.

I hope she was able to imagine mine and Stephanie's children and what our family would look like. Even though my kids did not have the same sweet introduction to their grandmother as my nephew did, they know my mom as if she were still here today. They make her famous brownies with chocolate chips, topped with confectioners' sugar. They enjoy the same songs she sang to me as a child. They have a love for chickens, like she did. And they all have a picture of her next to their bed.

My mom lives on in their smiles, in their eyes, and in their hearts.

At 12:30 a.m. on December 3, 2003, my mom's breathing became very shallow, taking a short breath about every 20 seconds. Her face looked relaxed. Her eyes were softly closed, and she seemed to be free of pain. Everyone had gone home for the day, and it was just me and Stephanie sitting there next to my mom. We stepped out of the room for a minute, as we often did, to collect ourselves and clear our heads. Ironically, I found myself sitting in the common area with an old high school friend whose mom was also dying just one room over. As we were both losing a big part of ourselves, we embraced our connection to the past. I took a quick break from our conversation to check in on my mom and tell her again that I loved her.

It would be for the last time.

Several minutes passed, and I noticed she had not taken a breath. I notified the nursing staff, and they confirmed that her heart was filled with all our love and was no longer beating. It was official.

My mom had died.

The funeral was a special celebration of her life. She would have never believed the hundreds of people that showed up. Her casket was carried on the shoulders of police officers in my department, as well as escorted by them to the cemetery.

This is what family does.

They lift you up when you cannot lift yourself.

My mom was pretty adamant that she did not want anyone crying over her grave. She used to say, "While my body may be buried in the ground, that is not where I am." My mom reminded us that she would be the pinch in our hearts, the bird in a tree, the sunshine through the clouds, the extra chocolate in a brownie, and the love we share with each other.

In the 20 years since her passing, I have only been to the cemetery a few times. She was right; all I found there was sadness and grief. I choose to see her in the eyes of my children. I feel her in the kindness from strangers. I hear her in the snap, crackle, and pop of the occasional bowl of Rice Krispies™. It was her favorite breakfast.

Rest in peace, Mommy.
I hope you are proud of the man,
police officer, husband, and father I have become.
You will forever be my guiding light,
and I will forever be your Bunz Bear.

Stephanie and I were married in October 2004. We sold the townhouse and the "green couch" I bought from my sister, shortly after we got married. To begin our incredible journey together, we bought a beautiful, starter house in a wooded development and called it home for the first seven years of our marriage. We made great friends, traveled the world and were blessed with our first two children. I was still caring for my grandmother, Ge, who moved from a freestanding home in a retirement village to a full-service complex where she thrived for many more years to come. It was not a conventional "nursing home" but rather a spa vacation for the elderly. Picture a cruise-ship type lifestyle for the last 10 to 15 years of life.

In 2010, following the births of our first two children, our family moved into the home we live in now. Ge passed in 2012, and sadly, never got to meet our third and final child who was born in 2013. Stephanie proved to be my everything. Beyond being the perfect mother, she became my mentor, my conscience, my money manager and my gravitational pull back to center when I get too close to the edge. She is my guardian angel, my first and last call of the day, and ultimately one of the four reasons I am alive today. She has always given me hope that tomorrow will be okay, and in the darkest moments of my life, she is always that beacon of light.

Stephanie is an accomplished corporate marketer who was the brains behind many brands like Swedish Fish, Sour Patch Kids, Certs, Mentos and other popular candies. However, she is best known for being a sexual health expert that includes her work with the Trojan™ Brand and First Response™.

She holds two patents for her part in the and creation of the Trojan™ Vibes and lube products. After 20 years of corporate dominance, Stephanie left her job and started her own marketing consulting company that supports businesses in many sectors of consumer goods, and she continues to be a sought-out expert in sexual health. She was recruited by one of her biggest clients and is now the vice president of marketing for Twinings North America. After three years out on her own, being hired to come in-house was the best accolade an entrepreneur could get.

From the condom queen to the tea lady!

As for our relationship, I know I have failed Stephanie in many ways, from being absent, even when I am in the room, to my lack of affection and refusal to dance at formal affairs. She still claims "false advertising" since that is how we met. I hope someday I can be a fraction of the partner to her that she has been to me.

Marriage is not easy.

However, it is important for both individuals to take accountability for their failures, while showing grace to each other and being willing to express both in a shared "no judgment zone."

Which leads us here, 20 years later. Through all of my ups and downs, Stephanie has put up with a lot of shit. She has had every right to walk away many times over the course of our relationship, but she has courageously chosen to see something in me that I struggle to see in myself. She has found a way to love me when I cannot love myself. Stephanie and our kids are my greatest blessing.

They are my everything.

Alex, our oldest, is my doppelganger. He thrives on the baseball field and is a NASCAR enthusiast with racing knowledge that even professional analysts can learn from. He plans to be a NASCAR engineer and is directing his studies to accomplish that goal. Zack is a beautiful soul with a kind and caring heart. He also thrives on the baseball field and wants to be an aerospace engineer or a woodworker building furniture. He also loves nature and quiet time to think. Danielle is a social butterfly that oozes joy from every part of her. She loves to ride horses and is an avid softball player and budding gymnast. All three are avid skiers, and we share winter weekends together on the mountain making memories.

I take the time to enjoy every possible moment with my kids. They are what wake me up in the morning—literally and figuratively. They are what drive me to be my best, the reason I continue to do my part to make the world a better place to live. I do it for others, too, but family first, always. My grandparents and my mom are "the house that built me."

Thank you, Miranda Lambert!

Your chart-topping song personifies my family who came before me. As for my marriage to Stephanie and our three kids, they are the house I built. Someday I will write another book chronicling my life with Stephanie and the pride and joy I feel for my kids and their accomplishments. I will write about the second half of my life and how it all turned out. Today, I can only imagine and dream about what the future holds, and I don't want to spoil the stories up to this point. So, for now, I will leave you with this:

Cherish your family,
the great loves of your life,
past and present.
They are everything!

CHAPTER FOURTEEN
Friends are Family We Choose

E ducation and experience are the foundation that build one's brain, but relationships and connection are the foundation that build one's heart. In the movie The Wizard of Oz, the Scarecrow and the Tin Man represent the cognitive and emotional centers of Dorothy. Both need to flourish for the individual to thrive. In the same way, our personal relationships are at the center of our emotional quotient.

Surround yourself with people who will love you, inspire you, and test you but who will also be there to catch you when you cannot catch yourself. As a police officer, being vulnerable enough to let others in was the hardest thing I ever had to do. No matter how thick or how high I built the walls around me, there were friends who broke through to the other side, and I will forever hold them tight and never let them go.

In the early years of my life, my bio-family was the center point of my socialization, as it is for many. I did not have many school friends, but I did enjoy time with neighborhood kids, like Jason and Andy. Together, we played backyard football and Army (because no one plays Navy and Air Force). And we made audiotape recordings of our "radio station." There was also Josh, a neighborhood and synagogue friend who I enjoyed skiing with on school and Township Recreation Department trips. Josh and I grew closer when we both joined the Rescue Squad. Up through high school and even into college, Josh remained one of my best friends. Before either of us started driving, we installed CB radios in our rooms and chatted, like two truckers on the open road. We parted ways after he moved to California for work. Sometime later, Josh was arrested, charged, and incarcerated for being a "Herb."

Yup, my best friend was caught diddling kids.

While he was a significant part of my early life and chosen family, Josh, ultimately, violated my trust with his lies, deceit, and abhorrent behavior. Choice is a powerful tool, and he is no longer a part of my life.

What a scumbag!

Adam, my lifelong best friend, who I introduced you to earlier, is a part of my heart and soul. We are best friends—family! From childhood antics to policing the beach together, the best moments Adam and I have shared are weddings, births, and funerals—life's most precious moments. I am also the proud godfather to his son. My kids refer to Adam and his wife as their uncle and aunt, and his kids refer to Stephanie and me in the same way. I look up to Adam, professionally, as he is a major with the Maryland State Police, and I could not be prouder of who he is as a husband, a father, a son, a friend, and a brother.

Adam, I love you, brother!

He and I have also shared experiences that include alcohol, girls, and guns. But for the record, we were **not** the ones who pointed his dad's gun at a passing middle-school girl from the second story window of his parents' residence, yelling inappropriate things. It was another kid, and even though Adam and I were innocent, that incident put both of our careers in law enforcement in jeopardy. It completely took a "cop job" off the table for the kid who did point the gun, which was very sad because his late father was on the job, and he wanted to continue the legacy.

When Adam and I were embarking into law enforcement, police jobs were extremely competitive. At the time, departments only accepted the best among us. The jobs were hard to get and easy to lose. Unlike today, there were at least 1,000 candidates for every position, and you had to be the best of the best and have no association with a troubled past of any kind. In recent years, following the *defund and defame* movement and lowering recruitment standards, the hiring process looks much different, but more on that later.

❦

From David G. to David L., there are many David's in my life. Those two, specifically, are a big part of who I am today. Both of their dads are on my Father's Day list. David L. is someone I met at a sleepaway camp when we were nine. As I mentioned, my mom sent me there for four weeks out of every summer. David L. and I were bunkmates until our final summer at the age of 14, and then years later, we found ourselves attending the same college.

Halfway through our freshman year, we became bunkmates again for two semesters. To this day, David L. is one of my closest friends. I was proud to stand with him at both his weddings (overachiever!) and during the birth of his girls. While life has put some distance between us, we still talk regularly and enjoy catching up over life's biggest moments.

I am proud of your recent transformation and newfound confidence, DL! It is never too late to recognize that which suppressed us in life's previous chapters, so long as we use those experiences to understand what we want in the present and chart a new path forward that is more consistent with who we want to become in the future. Resiliency is at its core.

⁓

My friend Tammy is my compass. Like Adam, she has been a part of my heart and soul since we met freshman year in high school at a youth group event. She and I also went to college together. Tammy and her family have been a steady example of everything that is right in this world. Like every other family, they have contended with their own challenges, but it is in the way they handle those challenges that I admire them. They are all love, all the time, and the love Tammy shares with me, as a friend, is the type of love you only share with family. After a recent weekend together, combining her family and mine, our kids now share that same admiration for each other.

It was an honor to witness and celebrate Tammy's oldest daughter's bat mitzvah together, a Jewish rite of passage that will forever connect our families through the *"Priestly Blessings."* After 33 years of having Tammy in my life and with the help of a few others, I have begun to love again. And I have *finally* learned the following lesson:

Show love, and you shall receive it.

Allow yourself to be loved, and you will be able to love in return.

The caveat: You must learn to love yourself first.

⁓

And lastly, there is Tom. Tom and I met in our college fraternity. I was his pledge master, and at first, we did not care for each other very much. Throughout our college experience, however, we grew to tolerate and even enjoy each other's company. It wasn't until after college that we truly grew close, like brothers. There are many stories to tell, but nothing made me realize how important Tom is to me as when my mom passed.

Tom was actively serving in the Bush '43 Presidential Administration and was on assignment in Iraq as the communications director to Ambassador Bremmer. Following my mom's funeral, we hosted a reception at her house for family and friends. This is known in the Jewish tradition as *Shivah*. It was a revolving door of people and food. There was one certain knock at the door and a certain food delivery, however, that stood out.

I answered the door, like I had several times that day. The delivery guy had a confused look on his face. He was carrying an unreal amount of Italian food.

"Are you David," he asked.

"Yes," I replied.

"I think this may be a prank, but the charge card cleared. So, we made the food, and now I am delivering it."

I nodded in curiosity.

"It's a delivery for the Berez family in memory of Linda Berez from someone named Tom," he added.

"Why would you think this was a prank," I asked.

The driver smiled and continued, "The guy who called in the order said he was calling from Iraq and was playing fake battle sounds in the background. We thought it was in bad taste, and we were not sure what to do, but as I said, the payment cleared."

After a much-needed laugh, I felt obligated to explain and thank him for the delivery. The driver said it was the best delivery-driver story ever and was honored to be part of it.

Food delivery driver street cred—sweet!

Tom called me a few hours later to extend his condolences "in person" and to confirm we received the food. Knowing his Italian roots, I would joke about the true priority of his call. Was he really calling out of compassion, or did he simply want to make sure there was enough food and we were all well fed?

In all seriousness, I know Tom was devastated that he could not be by my side. Being stationed in a faraway land, he has mentioned often that he never felt farther from home than he did when my mom died. The food delivery and the good laugh I got changed the mood in the house, even if it was only for a short period of time. The story was shared to all those who gathered. It lightened the tension and sadness, creating a moment of joy and connection. Resiliency has taught me that joy and sadness cannot coexist simultaneously. So, the more joy you allow in, the more sadness you will push out. Even in your darkest moments, you can find light.

From then on, Tom was considered family.

I have enjoyed supporting Tom through his professional and personal journey. From politics to television news to marriage and children, I could not be prouder of his accomplishments. Tom has become my brother, my mentor, and my conscience. He will always give it to me straight, whether I like it or not. I always listen to what he has to say because he has never steered me wrong. We support each other in every way possible. He and Adam serve as two halves of one whole in my life, and no one knows me better than them. Tom has challenged me to grow like no one else I know. His faith in God is something I wish I had. He is genuine at every level, inspiring me every day and pushing me to be the best version of myself.

I would not be who I am without him.

My friends and family have seats at the head of the table for my personal board of directors. I continue to add seats for friends, like Tim and

Michele, who have been a constant source of friendship for the past seven years. Friends are definitely the family we choose. As for me, I have chosen well, and I am eternally grateful that they, too, see worth in choosing me.

CHAPTER FIFTEEN
Tales From the Crypt

W hile 9/11 was the highest profile incident of my career and an experience that would shape the rest of my life both personally and professionally, I have many other stories that influenced who I am today. There are too many to capture in a single book, but I would like to share some of my favorites with you in these pages. Some are funny. Some are sad. Some are insightful, and some are examples of why being a cop is like having a front row seat at The Greatest Show on Earth. No matter what each story represents, they all hold a special place in my heart. While the stories I collected as a volunteer on the Rescue Squad are mostly consumed with horrific images of tragedy—blood, guts, and gore, my law enforcement stories are primarily of triumph and leadership at a young age. These experiences built my confidence, proving to be a recipe for future success in emergency service.

Squad Captain

I was just 19 years old when the Rescue Squad volunteers elected me as the agency's captain (agency line officer behind the chief and deputy chief—call sign 912) for the 1994 calendar year. I never held a lower position, with the exception of being a leader with the Cadet Corps. I had all the training but none of the experience to be a line officer. While I was a crew chief of a duty shift, in charge of individual calls, I was never in a position of incident command. That all changed on a cool January afternoon, just one week into my new position. The tones sounded from my pager. The dispatcher advised there was a multi-vehicle crash on Dutch Neck Road at the Hickory Corner Road intersection—an initial count of six injured passengers. One driver was reportedly trapped and another was suffering severe physical trauma. For the first time as a line officer, I responded directly to the scene in my personal vehicle.

"912 dispatch … I will be responding."

Wow! That felt good!

I sent my next transmission, "912 dispatch, 10-97 (on-scene) with a two-car motor vehicle accident, multiple injuries and one trauma needing heavy rescue for extrication."

I was in full auto-pilot mode. It was like I was watching a really cool version of myself on the big screen. I radioed back, "912 dispatch, this may be a prolonged extrication. Please contact State Police for a Medivac. Dispatch fire as well and have them set up a landing zone at McGraw Hill."

Holy Shit!

This crash was the motherload of resources, and I was responsible for coordinating it all. When the dust cleared, I made the final radio call. "912 dispatch, all patients enroute to the hospital, and all rescue units are clear."

I had done it. I managed my way through a complete clusterfuck for the first time as an officer within the squad. All patients were successfully rescued, stabilized, and transported to higher medical care. More importantly, all of the EMT's, fireman, flight crew, and paramedics completed the call without injury to themselves. I grew so much from that incident. I was given much praise by folks I looked up to, and the success of the incident gave me the confidence to make a career out of being a first responder. This was the moment I knew I had arrived.

Surface Ice Rescue

One of the greatest experiences I had in EMS was at a Surface Ice Rescue class. This was a two-day training. Day one was in a classroom. Day two was at a nearby frozen lake. During the classroom portion of the course, we talked about theory, learned nomenclature of the equipment, and counted down the time to lunch and dismissal. The real magic happened on day two when we got to put the information learned on day one to use. That is, if we paid attention.

While I was a decent swimmer and a thrill seeker, I was never a big fan of confined spaces. I also had a fear of drowning, and I was not great with a snorkel, mask, and the equipment needed to breath under water. When it came my turn to gear up and put classroom theory into practical use, I squeezed into the rescue swimmer's red, dry suit. I tied the tether rope to my waist harness and strapped on the SCUBA tank with the (dreaded) mask and snorkel. I slithered across the ice and "fell" into the hole that simulated the ice breaking beneath me. I then swam beneath the surface of the ice in search of the rescue dummy simulating a trapped swimmer.

I expected the space under the ice to be dark, cold, and scary. I could not have been more wrong. While I was not able to see much through the murky water, it was bright, warm, and peaceful. I had never felt more dead and more alive at the same time. It was such a euphoric feeling; I literally forgot to search for the rescue dummy and, instead, soaked up the experience.

Pun intended.

After a little while, I felt a tug on my rescue rope. It was a reality check, a reminder to find my way out from under the ice. As I looked for the hole where I entered the water, I saw a bright light. Like a stud (and badass rescuer), I swam right to it. I gave a strong, final kick and expected to pop out of the water, but instead I hit my head fairly hard on the ice.

What the fuck just happened?

I started to feel around, but I was not able to find the hole.

Yup! The panic started to sink in.

I realized I was in trouble and much to my dismay, I tugged on the rope to signal to the instructors to pull me out. I felt like such a failure. I was pulled out from under the ice, and I could not get the mask and snorkel off fast enough. Once I calmed down, I was asked by the instructor to describe what happened. After answering him, he explained that the exit hole in the ice would be the dark circle, just like we were instructed in class.

Ugh!

You mean the same class I was more focused on lunch and dismissal? I had the opportunity to make a few more practice rescue attempts. All were completed successfully, and I passed the class. Yes, I am a certified underwater/surface ice rescue tech. However, I learned many lessons, other than just those taught in the classroom and under the ice. I learned that lunch was not that important and missing it would not be life threatening. However, having my priorities wrong could be.

I also learned to trust others with my safety when I failed myself. Most importantly, I learned that I could find peace, euphoria, and light in the darkest places. These are lessons I will forever carry forward for both my physical and mental health.

Seaside Park PD

As I moved into my policing career, I often connected with people who were in imminent danger, but more times than not, most citizen interactions were singular, non-life-threatening calls. There were also those interactions that were singular moments in an individual's ongoing relationship with law enforcement personnel. These interactions were not any less impactful than the other interactions that resulted in great stories.

My time spent at Seaside Park was filled with great interactions and experiences. From the locker room antics to leaving a dead fish in a paper bag under the driver's seat of the chief's car during one of the hottest Julys on record in New Jersey, I have many memories worth holding onto. There were foot pursuits down the boardwalk and breaking up fights at The Sawmill, a local boardwalk bar and restaurant. Two of the best jobs at the beach were the ATV and jet ski details. The worst was a standing traffic post.

Whoever was assigned to parking-ticket duty for the night was also assigned to drive the Cushman, a three-wheeled, three-speed manual vehicle maneuverable through urban environments. It is most commonly used by the NYPD Housing Unit. The best and most useful feature was the watertight trunk that held several bags of ice and up to 10 cases of beer. It was great for evidence storage until proper disposition of the items could be made. Gathering pre-shift ice and maintaining the chain of custody of the seized evidence was the responsibility of the assigned officer. It was also widely encouraged that the on-duty officer locked the trunk because the Cushman was unable to navigate sand and flipped easily.

Or so I have been told.

I connected with all kinds of people, but in a place like Seaside

Park, my greatest source of interactions was with tourists. I recall several nights when we would be called to an address where a party would be taking place at a rental property. We would arrive to an underage gathering that was fueled by alcohol and raging hormones of underage alcoholic beverage consumers. While one needs to be 21 years of age to purchase or consume adult beverages, one only needed to be 18 years old to rent a beach property. That said, for those who would do the latter, the former seemed to be a mere suggestion rather than a law.

Upon my arrival at the call, I knocked on the door and announced my presence. Half the attendees scattered out the back, while others hid in the bathrooms, some just remained present, trying to play it cool. When I asked to speak with the renter, the drunk dude who opened the door summoned the hottest girl at the party to try to win me over, hoping for a warning instead of a summons. I knew the game and welcomed it, but what the drunk dude at the door did not know was that it was just the leverage I needed. You see, I, too, was once a playa.

"Good evening, Ma'am. I am Officer Berez. We got a complaint of an underage party. If you cannot produce an adult that is legally allowed to consume the 15 cases of beer in this cooler on the porch, we will have to confiscate it."

"If the beer is confiscated, can we just get a warning," the inebriated woman replied.

"Yes. There will be no further problem," I said.

"Just curious," she asked. "What happens to all the beer at the end of the night?"

"Well, Ma'am," I answered, remaining surprisingly stoic. "It gets properly disposed of. If you have any concerns, you can join us at the 14th Street beach when we end our shift and help us with that."

It never failed!

Cops like me would end a party (complete with a bunch of sloppy, drunk dudes trying to get girls drunk in hopes of hooking up) and turn around and offer those same girls the opportunity to have a more respectable experience with another bunch of sloppy, drunk dudes trying to get girls drunk in hopes of hooking up. The only difference was that we were the knights in shining armor. We had badges and guns, and we had a higher CDI factor–Chicks **D**ig **It**!

Badge bunnies and holster sniffers are everywhere from the start of one's career to the finish. We are warned as far back as the police academy that the three Bs are the easiest way to lose your job: **B**ooze, **B**oobs, and **B**ucks. The booze gets the boobs; the boobs get the bucks, and you will lose your job and go right back to the booze.

Vicious cycle!!

Bathroom Break

One night, back in Seaside Park, I was assigned to a patrol car, and my best friend, Adam, was assigned to a foot post. Usually, about an hour into his assigned duty, I would pick him up, and we would drive around town together for most of our shift. It was great until the time he got caught off post.

I will never forget when the summer sergeant called for him on the radio, wondering why he was off post. To cover my best friend's ass, I answered the sergeant's call, advising him that I had picked him up for a bathroom break.

"Is he okay," the sergeant asked. "Because I have been on his post for two hours, and he has not been here. There must be something wrong."

Keeping up appearances, I replied, "In fact, there is sergeant. It must have been the chili he had for lunch. By the way, I have been looking for you for the last two hours to let you know but couldn't find you. I never thought to check the parking lot where the foot post guys go to hide."

Yup, that went about as well as you might think.

The very next shift I was easy to find, since *I* was the one assigned to my buddy's foot post. Those two summers at the shore came and went. I was happy to be a part of the Jersey Shore's revolving door.

East Windsor PD

Once I was hired as a full-time cop in East Windsor, it would be years before I would make my way back to Seaside Park. My first squad was like the Bad News Bears. One guy drove around in the shittiest car his wife could find. It was known as the "Mom Wagon." That way, he would be less likely to pick up chicks.

True story!

He crashed that car on the way home from a bar one night, nearly losing his life and taking another squad member with him in the process. His blood alcohol content (BAC) was over .40 percent. Due to his injuries, he spent weeks in the hospital and never did return to the job. Fortunately, the other officer did return to work. However, he retired (early) after going on a 30-day vacation in Florida to get sober. I should note that he just celebrated 10 years sober, and I am so proud of him and his success. He is also now a recovery coach managing a growing program.

Resilient!

My sergeant also retired early due to a psychological breakdown following 9/11. Just prior to his departure, he went on vacation in Key West, Florida. He sent us all pictures of himself at a drag show. He was dressed in nothing but feathers. Sarge returned with a new tattoo of upside-down chevrons and the words "Rouge Sarge" inked on him. The department sent him for a fit-for-duty test, and we never saw him again.

It is safe to assume he did not pass.

It was this same squad that followed each other into the sand pits with our patrol cars, and we all got stuck.

Yes, the entire shift buried their cars up to the frames for hours.

The neighboring town covertly covered our calls until we were able to get towed out.

Thanks, HPD and Macky's towing.

We owe you!

Our squad was comprised of "sandlot" style cops that were not proficient in policy or procedure. Because we did it "our way," we often found ourselves painting outside the lines, and everything we did turned to shit. However, there is no other group of cops I would rather be in the shit with. We had each other's backs and there was no way we would go home any other way than safe.

Well, safe and drunk.

Choir Practice

We held "choir practice" at least two mornings every week, if not after every shift. For those less familiar with choir practice, I suggest you read the book "Choir Boy" by Joseph Wambaugh. In short, "choir practice" is the art of group decompression through self-medication in the most secluded area of town, usually behind an abandoned building where the entire squad can cleanse their conscience and the workday with alcohol.

This "practice" allows the brain to quiet itself, so that one can sleep through the sunniest part of the day, when the neighbor to the left is sure to be cutting the lawn and the neighbor to the right is fixing the throttle on his Harley Davidson (with short pipes), and the Girl Scouts are banging down your door trying to sell you cookies, effectively ignoring the sign on the bell that reads: "Do not press."

Patrol Outtakes

So many of the calls I took with my old partner, Bart, bring a smile to my face. We were friends inside and outside of work, sharing many common interests. We never had a shortage of laughs or beer to pour over. Many of my experiences as a cop are shared with him, and to this day, we reminisce over many of these tales that I am sharing with you. So, it only felt right, when deciding what anecdotes were to make the cut, that I consult with him. Here are some of the outtakes:

There was a special needs senior citizen named David who rode his bike everywhere he went. He had a bottle of Diet Coke strapped to the book rack, like a rocket booster. He was addicted to caffeine and rode around, like the Energizer Bunny at all hours of the day and night.

David and his wife had regular domestic disputes because the caffeine overdose would make the 70-year-old horny, and she would have none of it. We would often bring him back to the station to "question him" about the fights with his wife.

He always denied it.

One night, Bart placed David's hand on the computer printer, pretending it was a lie detector.

"Why were you arguing with your wife, David," Bart asked.

Again, David denied it.

In fun, one of us printed the words "You're lying!" on a single sheet of paper from that printer. Not long afterward, David put his head down and confessed. He was a sweet man but needed to lay off the sodas.

WWII Rifle

One of the scarier calls Bart and I responded to together was an old guy who lost his shit inside his home. He was an Alzheimer's patient who was threatening his wife, along with the two of us with an old, World War II rifle with a bayonet attached.

It was sad, really.

The old man felt captive in his home and, while holding his wife hostage, was "fighting his way back to his unit." It took us hours to get him to surrender. I will never forget when he first started hitting the storm door with the gun, and we all thought he was shooting at us. To this day, I cannot believe that none of us shot back at him.

Midnights

In police work, we are guided by a hierarchy of rules from the Constitution, state law, attorney general guidelines, local ordinances and the catch-all department policy and procedures manual. Much of it is common sense, but there are always a few head scratchers. One popular question among new officers is, "Where did that policy come from?" The best answer I ever heard was, "Midnight shift, kid ... midnights."

This could not be more on point.

For example, if you were on the job in the late 90s and into the early 2000s, you likely had the pleasure of driving a Chevy Caprice pursuit-rated police car with an LT1 motor. For those who don't geek out over engines, imagine taking a highly tuned Corvette engine, transmission, and exhaust package and putting it into your grandmother's full-size sedan. It was the most badass machine on four wheels, but as awesome as these patrol cars were, there was always room for improvement.

So, of course, it was nightshift, early spring, and the weather was starting to turn for the better. There was a newly constructed highway in town that became known as the Bypass. The roadway is a limited access highway, relatively straight, and 3.8 miles long. So, what do a few bored, gearhead cops do on a quiet mid-week nightshift?

Exactly what you think.

Open the hood, remove the intake limiting air filter, flip the filter box so the intake is wide open, and throttle up to see what this beast of a patrol car is made of! I recall a maxed-out speed of 133 mph but only because we ran out of road. We made several runs, competing for the highest speeds and fastest times. No one crashed. No one got hurt, and my partner, Bart, ended up with the bragging rights.

No surprise there.

So, when reading the department policy and procedure manual and the new kids ask why there is a policy that prohibits modifying a patrol car, as that seems like common sense, the answer is, *"Nightshift."*

There were many shenanigans over the years that included pushing our cruisers to the limits. Most of the time, there was no exciting ending to the stories, however, others ended in blown engines, dropped transmissions, or a catastrophic mechanical failure that left a trail of parts, like cookie crumbs, halfway down the highway.

Great job Skippy!

Then there was the total loss of Car 17. It literally went up in flames. For future reference, I suggest not parking a Ford Crown Vic on dried hay in the median for several hours. That shit WILL catch fire. The visual of my squad mate, Lee, standing next to the car-b-que, holding the oxygen bag and smoking a cigarette will be forever ingrained in my memory.

Cabinet Under the Sink

One of the most memorable calls for service was a foul odor coming from an Airstream trailer. The dispatcher advised she had asked the caller if they noticed anything unusual, and the caller explained that they were not able to see into the trailer because the windows were covered with flies. For anyone who has been in the emergency service profession, you know that is not a good sign, and it is probably time to prepare yourself for a scene that will make the producer of a horror movie squirm.

The stench was unlike anything I have ever encountered in my life. We knocked on the door of the trailer. We were greeted by an elderly gentleman who looked surprised to see us. Frankly, he did not appear happy about it either. We learned he and his wife had been living there for years when she had fallen ill. He was dedicated to her care but did not trust the "system." So, he took care of her alone, the best he knew how.

Time passed and his wife's condition deteriorated. We found her "living" in a cabinet underneath the sink inside the trailer. She was covered in feces and had a very weak and thready pulse, as low as 20 beats per minute. The woman had maggots coming out of every natural and unnatural opening of her body. This was a hazmat scene like I have never experienced during any other part of my emergency service career.

After the EMS crew properly suited up in Tyvek onesies and respirator masks, the woman was removed and transported to the hospital. She was literally being eaten alive from the inside out by maggots.

She did not survive.

If I recall correctly, her husband was criminally charged, but did not live long enough to stand trial.

Half-a-Head Fred

I won't ever forget half-a-head Fred who attempted to die by suicide, using a shotgun to blow his head off. When Fred pulled the trigger, he took out his lower jaw and the side of his face. Fred's lower lip was plastered to the ceiling. There were teeth everywhere and one of us unknowingly stepped on his tongue when we entered the room. We could not believe this man was still alive, able to walk to the ambulance on his own two feet. Fred died soon after from infection.

The Man Who Kept His Word

Over the course of my career, I crossed paths with all types of people. I also conducted many types of investigations, stemming from many different situations. Some were funny. Some were sad and traumatic, while others were just plain bizarre. I will never forget my first shift as acting supervisor of my squad. I was called to the lobby of the police station to meet with an individual who specifically asked to see a supervisor. My initial thought was, "Wow! That's me!"

It quickly turned to a pucker-factor moment. When someone waltzes into the station to speak with a boss, it is usually because they want to complain about an interaction with another police officer. It was my first time as a "boss," and the last thing I wanted to do was start an Internal Affairs complaint.

Not a good look.

So, I checked my gig line, cleared my throat, and walked out to the lobby with authority. I was greeted by a 60-something-year-old black man who looked sad, tired, and a bit disheveled. I figured one of our cops gave him a hard time or maybe even wrote him a ticket on a traffic stop, and he felt some level of discrimination. I had the guy all sized up and was ready to hear his version of the incident, a thousand excuses running through my head to smooth it over.

"Good afternoon, sir," I said, maintaining an authoritative stance, while extending a gentle, open hand. "I'm David, and I am the officer in charge. How can I help you today?"

"I killed my girlfriend, and I am turning myself in," he replied in a flat tone with no emotion, as if he were telling me the sky was blue.

"Okay," I chuckled. "Never heard that one before. How can I help you?"

I initially thought it was a stupid joke most people open with when talking to a cop. The man repeated himself, "I recently killed my girlfriend, and I want to turn myself in."

I quickly recognized that this was not an awkward one-liner, and the individual was either a Signal 47 (mental patient) or a cold-blooded killer. In case he was not crazy and was actually confessing to a crime, I read the man the Miranda warnings. He advised that he understood his rights.

"Where and when did this happen? And why do you believe your girlfriend is dead," I asked.

The man told me he stabbed her at his apartment in North Jersey earlier that morning and then dismembered her body, leaving all of the parts in the bathtub to bleed out.

"Should I continue to describe why I think she is dead," he asked.

"I don't think that will be necessary," I chuckled.

I ended the conversation, so any further interrogation would be fresh and untainted. However, I could not help myself.

"Why did you do it? Were you defending yourself?"

"Hell no! She was nagging me for days, and I just couldn't take it anymore. I told her if she kept up her shit, I would kill her and chop her up into pieces. She wouldn't quit, and I'm a man of my word," he explained. "I am sad to see her go, but I will not miss the nagging."

There was not much over the course of my career that left me speechless, but in that moment, I literally had nothing. The only thing I could say to the guy was, "I respect a man who keeps his word."

Probably not my finest moment.

Before long, the man was picked up by the investigating agency. On his way out, he thanked me for being understanding and for not judging him.

If he only knew. Ha!

If you just laughed, you've been in this business too long. For the rest of you, allow me to explain.

Dark humor is how we survive the day.

That senseless homicide was only second to the Zampini case. I was the first responding officer on that call and one of the lead investigators. The suspect killed his girlfriend because she would not get up to get him the TV remote control. So, instead of getting off his lazy ass to get it himself, he got up to grab a carving knife from the kitchen and proceeded to stab the shit out of his girlfriend. He then tried to hide the woman's body underneath the couch cushions. Let me just say, it was an easy game of hide and seek. The guy pleaded guilty and later died in prison.

Trailer Park Soap Opera

I always preferred the midnight shift over the day shift. There were no bosses looking over my shoulder, and the police work was much more my style. We were much more likely to have great encounters, like those at the local trailer park. Butchy was a local guy who lived in said trailer park. He looked it, too. Butchy was the second drunkest guy in the park, next to Tom, formerly a five-dollar an hour employee of a bakery called The Cakery.

One morning, Tom went into work and opened the door, like he had done a thousand times before. Only this time, the place exploded. Whomever locked up the night before, forgot to turn the gas oven off. Tom got a $1 million payout and became the richest, drunkest guy in the trailer park, out pacing Butchy by a lot!

Butchy won a different type of lottery. He married Linda, the hottest chick in the trailer park, which is not saying much. She also had the most teeth on the block. Butchy and Linda had a child together. His name was Danny. Butchy and Linda fought regularly, and we responded often. As a result, we got to know them all well. We all watched Danny grow up.

Quite often, the fights were over another drunk friend—Tom or another guy named Abi. Abi was about 20 years younger, only a few years older than Danny. Linda and Abi were known to share moments of private "intimacy" in public settings, and the police were called in to be the buzzkill. These images stuck with us for the rest of our lives.

Trauma of a different kind!

Years later, Abi got sober and got a job parking cars at a hotel in Princeton, New Jersey. I would see him a few times a year, and he was always so proud to tell me his number of sober days. He went back to school and is now doing IT work for a great company.

Unfortunately, Butchy was killed while trying to stumble across a major highway in town with an alcohol level that should have killed him before the vehicle that ran him over. Linda and Danny continued to reside together, which in the absence of Butchy and Abi, had an incestual relationship of their own. I will never forget arriving at their "No tell motel" room they called home for a domestic dispute. Danny answered the door, and Linda asked, "Who is it?"

"It's the cops," Danny yelled.

"Whatever you do, don't tell 'em your name, Danny," Linda yelled back. We all had to pause and laugh out loud, including Danny, himself.

There are Aliens on the Front Lawn

Mrs. Baboo was a middle-aged woman of Indian or Pakistani descent. She had a mental health diagnosis that went undiagnosed. Mrs. Baboo was delusional and often saw things that weren't there, specifically little green monsters she thought were spies for the government. She would call to report these alien creatures, and we would have to go out and calm her fears, several times per week.

Over time her compliance weakened, and it got to the point where we needed to get creative. So, one day my partner, Bart, made her a tin foil hat, explaining that she should wear it when walking around outside to block the radio signals and tracking devices. The enlightenment in her face was priceless, and she wore it for many days.

I love Bart.

We saw the job (and the world) through a similar lens, and we worked well together. Some time went by. We hadn't received any calls from Mrs. Baboo regarding the little green men, but one day it happened. The call came in and we responded with the usual eye roll, a slight giggle, and the rhetorical, "You have got to be fucking kidding me!"

What happened next could not have been better scripted in a Hollywood film. Upon our arrival at the home, we observed a well-known, local drug-fueled human wrecking ball dressed in a green tracksuit, eating the wires out of the Comcast cable box on the front lawn of the Baboo residence.

She never trusted us again!

What Can You Get for $25?

Who can forget the local perverts? There was Kyjack, the peeping Tom, who pleasured himself while staring into the windows of people's homes. There was Christopher, a 19-year-old mama's boy who was addicted to porn and displayed his ejaculates in Mason jars on his windowsill. I will also never forget Frosty Buck, a local prostitute who traversed the Twin Rivers area on her roller skates, wearing short shorts and leg warmers, like she just rolled out of an 80's film.

For $25, you got it all!

There was the murder of Jesse Unger, the first slaying where the victim and the alleged killer met online, using America Online. Jesse Unger, George "Chip" Hemenway, and a local 15-year-old boy met in a gay men's chat room and after a few weeks of online flirting, decided to get together in person. They rendezvoused at Hemenway's home in the middle of the night. During the sex-capade, Hemenway shot and killed Unger and solicited the boy to help dispose of the body in a rolled-up tarp. This case was a first of its kind using computer data warrants to get information from internet providers and AOL. It started the conversation regarding privacy and digital technology.

The Escape Artist

Another infamous case was the politically-motivated graffiti on the Route 133 bypass, the same roadway we used to race on. The limited access highway had sound barriers from end to end that served as a suspect's personal spray-paint canvas for years. The graffiti ranged from swastikas to antisemitic verbiage, from political messages to disdain for the local mayor. And when I say "graffiti," I mean to say the artist used a 10-foot panel per letter and a long sentence could read a mile long—literally. Incident after incident, and no arrest was made. There were a few folks we were suspicious of, however, there was no evidence linking the criminal mischief to anyone in particular. After a year or so with no leads, the department set up a task force to monitor the wall in the nighttime hours with three teams of two officers per night. Two of the teams were fixed surveillance and one team was a roving patrol. The fixed surveillance ranged from sitting in an unmarked (undercover) car with binoculars, lying in wait in a field or a marsh that was adjacent to the affected walls on the highway. The operation was like that of a Delta Force team or a sniper hunting the Vietcong, all to catch a nut with a spray can. After another year with no arrest or even a suspect, we shut down the operation.

The "artist" had gone dark.

A week later, wouldn't you know it? He struck again. Leadership was incensed. They refused to fire up another full-blown operation, however, nightshift was required to document patrols of the roadway three times per shift. The goal being, if he were to hit again, we would catch the graffiti before it was reported by the public. If it was missed, we were sure to get a day off.

That happened more than once.

Off the Grid

I have so many great stories over the 20 years that I served the East Windsor Community. The town, itself, was part commercial, part Beverly Hillbillies, part low-income garden apartments, part McMansions and everything in between. We had two trailer parks—Shady Rest and Crestfield Acres. Both represented every stereotype you may have of such a community.

Crestfield Acres was like something out of the twilight zone. It was truly a mobile home park where National Lampoon's Christmas Vacation's Cousin Eddie's rig would have been considered the high-end unit. And, like Cousin Eddie's loo, everyone's shitter must have been full because most residents relieved themselves at will around the community. If that weren't bad enough, there was only one power line coming in from the street with one meter on a pole. Every trailer was tapped into the main line, essentially getting free electricity, and there was a maze of hazardous wires all over the place. The residents were an odd collection of reclusive individuals with a varying array of mental health issues and an "off-the-grid" mentality, distrusting government and public services.

NL3

There were certain places in town, like the old livestock auction and the former National Lead site that became a local hang out for on-duty cops looking to shrink out of public view for a bit. This was the place you could let your guard down, write reports, call your wife or girlfriend or both and take the occasional snooze.

The National Lead location, otherwise known as NL3, was actually an old Superfund site polluted with hazardous materials and a series of abandoned buildings. It was an attractive nuisance for followers of Weird New Jersey magazine, especially on weekend nights when the ghost-hunting freaks came out.

During the day, however, it was home to UPS drivers, the power company, truck drivers, and the unfaithful who were mostly area co-workers engaged in extramarital affairs. Squeezed between two utility trucks on a union break, you could often find a high-end car with windows fogged up, bouncing like a hooptie in an '80s breakdance video on MTV.

Regardless of the company kept in this particular location, it was known to be a safe place to take a deep breath and decompress as you studied the inside of your eyelids. Everyone parked back there was doing the same thing, except the overachievers in the high-end car who, incidentally, were the best ones to keep a secret and the most hypervigilant for any unwanted visitors. The site has since been repurposed and is no longer accessible.

RIP, NL3!

What happened at NL3, stayed at NL3, and it was usually some legendary shit!

Animal Control

While the stories of yesteryear are memories that will last a lifetime, there was also an eclectic cast of characters. I will change the names so as not to offend, but the characterizations are true to form. First, there was Norm. Norm was the township's Animal Control Officer. He was the guy who graduated high school in the 70s and really wanted to be a cop, but for one reason or another, likely the psych exam, he did not get the job.

Norm settled for the animal control officer position, but always pretended to play the cop. To Norm's credit, he was one of the first ACOs in New Jersey, and he set the standard. He was certified in every animal situation known to man and was really good at his job. It was just really hard to take him seriously because he took himself so seriously. He donned a formal Class-A uniform or a Top-Gun-style flight suit every day at work. He rolled around in a take-home puppy truck with lights, but no siren. He also wore a police-style leather belt with all sorts of tools attached, including an empty gun holster.

Rumor had it, he once had a .38 caliber-style gun used to subdue rabid animals but got caught using it as a sign of authority, and it was taken from his regular possession. If there was a need to subdue an animal, he could request permission to get it from locked storage or have a police officer respond to assist. Until his retirement, he never gave up hope that someday he could officially carry a gun again.

The Salty Sergeant

Every agency has a salty sergeant, and East Windsor was no exception. Sergeant "Tackleberry" was as salty a sergeant that ever was! Rumor has it that he was on the job for somewhere near 120 years and had no fucks left to give. The legend of Sergeant Tackleberry involves his shotgun. We all had one center-mounted in a vertical position between the front seats of our patrol cars. Tackleberry's was cooler because it doubled as an ashtray. Being that he was never without a smoke in the car, he would flick his cigarette ash into the top of the barrel. Watching him use that thing to put down deer was always entertaining. The amount of ash and soot that preceded the birdshot was hysterical, except for that one time he rolled up on a struck deer near Anchor Park.

There was an officer already on scene. He was concerned about dispatching the animal because there were citizens standing nearby. Tackleberry was still sitting in the driver's seat of his patrol car. With his car still in drive, the passenger window rolled down, and a smoke dangling from his lips, he asked the patrolman to step aside. Sergeant Tackleberry shouldered the shotgun and put down the deer without ever stepping foot out of his car, shooting through the open passenger window. He then rolled up the window and drove away like that shit never happened. That fucking guy was as old school as they come.

Family Favorites

Part of being a sworn police officer is maintaining a level of confidentiality to protect the victims, the rights of the accused, and the system of justice we all have a responsibility to uphold. Another part is to protect family and friends from the good, the bad, and the extremely ugly that goes along with the job. So many of these stories I am telling for the first time. However, there are a few less traumatic experiences that my family loves for me to repeat. While these stories are funny, they are also the only connection my family had to my daily activities.

One day, I was driving eastbound on Etra Road, making my way through a rural section of town. Residents along this stretch ranged in age and background and did not have a full mouth of teeth between them. They couldn't have been more friendly, waving as I passed by with their meth-mouth smiles. One day, I saw an elderly man standing outside of his home on the Etra curve near Feldsher Road. He was frantically waving me down, hoping to get my attention. So, I pulled over and stopped to talk to him.

"Is everything okay," I asked.

"Everything is not okay," the man cried. "I need your help!"

The man went on to explain that there had been several deer struck at the hairpin curve in the road, and he knew exactly what the problem was and how to solve it.

"The road department recently placed a 'Caution: Deer Crossing' sign on the curve, and this is a real miscalculation," he said. "This is clearly not a safe location for deer to cross. The sign should be moved further up the road, away from the curve, where the deer are less likely to get hit."

This fucking guy was dead serious!

So, being the good community policing officer I was, I moved the sign. I am not sure I solved the problem, but the old man could not have been happier, and Rudolph the Red-nosed Reindeer lived to lead Santa's sleigh another Christmas.

Oh deer!

La Cucaracha

My kids like hearing about the late-night call made in response to a foul odor coming from an upstairs apartment. The building's power went out, and when we arrived on scene, we were invited into the home by the resident. My partner and I entered together. We followed the woman upstairs. Of course, none of these residences resembled a five-star resort, and you never knew what to expect.

The odor was strong, metallic, like a harsh cleaning chemical. As we traversed the steps, we crunched over what we thought were potato chips or some other garbage on the floor. When we inquired with the resident as to the smell she replied, "No worry, my friend. La Cucaracha."

My partner and I looked at each other in confusion, wiggling our hips a little in jest. Suddenly, the lights turned on, and we saw the smell. On the table was a variety of Raid™ products. We both paused and slowly looked down. We were frozen in our boots. Those were not potato chips we were walking on. The floor was covered in cockroaches, some of them squashed under the bottom of our boots. The last of the living dinosaurs scurried towards the walls, trying to escape the light. *My kids love this story!* They would dance to their version of "La Cucaracha," the Mexican Hat Dance, every time I told it. I still cringe at the thought.

While I can talk about my work stories now, I mostly held them beneath my vest, locked in a mental, emotional, and legal box. Our stories are a part of who we are, and when we can't share them with those who love us most, they will never have the full picture of our life. There will always be a bit of curiosity for the complete story of who we are as a person. Part of who we are will always be a mystery, and that can cause a breakdown in relationships. Sharing my complete story, including these tales from the professional crypt, will surely be part of bringing me closer to those who love me most.

The Letter

The story I want to leave you with is one of grace and gratitude in the face of tragedy and in a time of loss. In October of 2010, I responded to a medical call. An adult male was reported to have fallen down some stairs. I knew the family. The victim was the father of a high school classmate and neighborhood friend of mine. I found the man lying at the bottom of the staircase. His wife reported that he had fallen the entire flight, from the second floor to the main level where we were standing.

There were no visible injuries, and the patient was unresponsive. It looked like he had experienced some sort of medical emergency before the fall. I did my best to render aid but was unable to make much progress. Upon their arrival, EMS took over patient care. I turned to the man's wife, the mother of my neighborhood friend, to console her as she watched the love of her life slip away. Following the call, I learned that he had passed away from injuries resulting from his fall.

My heart was broken for the family.

A connection formed between her and I that night. The truth is I am still not sure who was consoling who. The grace that this woman showed me that night, allowing me to cry with her, is something I will never forget and forever embrace. It was the same grace that I gave her as a future widow.

On March 11, 2011, I received a card in my mailbox at work. It was from her. While I thought about that call often, I never did reach out to the family because it was too painful for me. It was one of those calls I needed to compartmentalize and store way back in the archives of my mind, never to be seen again. I was reluctant to open the card, but I did. To this day, it is one of my most treasured mementos from my career. Somehow, this woman knew I needed to hear these words:

David,

Your arrival to my home ... on the night of October 21, 2010 remains vivid in my memory. My husband Robert died from his injuries sustained in his fall down the steps. To me, that night you brought me the reassurance and comfort that the emergency would be handled. I will always remember your professionalism and compassion to me and Robert. When on the job and you need a cup of coffee or a kind word or thank you—my door is always open to you. Thank you and God bless you every day for your valuable service.

Fondly,
Carol

I reflect on Carol's card regularly as a reminder of the goodness in people, as well as the positive impact we can have when showing compassion and empathy. In the midst of this woman's loss, she held compassion and grace in her heart for someone else—for me. I learned so much from her, including how to face adversity. Most of all, I learned that love is the greatest of all emotions, and to always remember to bring empathy to every call for service. I look forward to sending Carol a copy of this book in the mail and having her read how she influenced and inspired the rest of my career and life.

Thank you, Carol!

CHAPTER SIXTEEN
A Cry for Help

I took the promotional exam four times during my career and was left on the top of the list twice without ever being promoted. The first time I took it, I failed the written test by one question. The second and third time I did well, respectively, placing third and fourth. The last time I took the exam, I failed.

I had not prepared for it at all.

The two times I made the list, promotions were made for those who placed higher than me and from there, the list died with me in the number one spot on both occasions. The second time there was an open sergeant's position, the agency opted not to fill it. If they actually wanted me to be a supervisor, they could have offered it to me.

Message received!

I never claimed to be the most insightful guy, but it was clear to me I had gone as far as I could in my career with the police department. The powers that be were not going to let me succeed, professionally, as a supervisor or beyond. I am not one to point fingers and play the victim. I take full ownership when I fuck up. However, this blatant use of force to subvert my career was personal.

Trust me.

The agency where I worked suffered from many layers of failed leadership. That failure in leadership manifested in failed working relationships, and those failed relationships extended as far as my family. I learned that even my wife was disliked by my boss because she won a washer's tournament at his home, and it was taken as a sign of disrespect. I was told she should have let my boss win. Another leader feared I could do better than him, and that the reputation I was building as a proactive street cop was going to put his reputation in the shadows. Therefore, both individuals purposefully held me back. While I don't want to give them the satisfaction of breaking me, they were instrumental in my mental health breakdown, having succeeded at killing my career. When those in leadership positions fail to lead, they dishonor the family name on their chest and the agency name on their sleeve.

Though an official promotion was not my fate as a police officer, I was a squad leader, the officer in charge of my platoon. I served as a drug recognition expert (DRE), traffic officer, DARE instructor, and many other specialties throughout my career. I was successful and excelled in making the most arrests year after year, as well as taking into custody the most DUIs in department history. I was known to everyone in the community, from business owners to hotel managers, residents to schoolteachers, and neighborhood kids to neighborhood menaces. The good folks knew I would be the first one on scene to help in their time of need and the criminals knew I'd be the first one there to hold them accountable for their misdeeds.

I had earned the respect of my colleagues and the citizens of my community. So, while I was stuck on the bottom rung of the promotion ladder, and there were some who did not want to see my professional career progress, I was still able to make a significant contribution to the agency and town. Today, I am at peace with that.

In the summer of 2018, eighteen-and-a-half years into my policing career, I became complacent and bored. That is not a good combination.

Complacency plus boredom kills.

I was cutting corners, writing lazy reports, not checking my gear, and constantly getting called out for all of the above. For my entire career, I was possibly the most proactive cop in the department and always the first on scene. I took on every bit of work I could. I came in for overtime every time it was offered. I was the first to show up and the last to leave. Well into my 18th year, I was lucky to make it to roll call on time. I stopped working out before shift, and if something was not required or ordered, I didn't do it.

Looking back, it was a cry for help.

I was drowning and screaming out for a lifeline. No one heard me, and no one cared. I wondered how I had gone from hero to zero, and no one even asked why. How did they not see it?

No one was listening!

In 2021 Demi Lovato released a song titled, *"Anyone."* The first time I heard her sing it live on television, I fell to my knees, and I cried. The lyrics expressed exactly how I felt on the inside. If you haven't heard the song, I encourage you to find it, and listen to it. Listen for the pain in Lovato's voice when she sings it. That was me.

Nobody's listening to me.

Why wasn't anyone listening?

I spent the greater part of the last nine months of my career sleeping through nightshift, hiding through dayshift, and loathing being at work. I was miserable at home, fighting with my wife and falling out of favor with my kids. I watched it all happen in front of me, like I was watching a movie.

I saw it.

I heard it.

I felt it.

I just could not stop it.

The noise in my head was loud, and all I saw was darkness, hate, and sadness. I could no longer feel joy, and I could no longer feel or give love.

I was done!

One Thursday evening in February 2019, while at work, driving my patrol car, I noticed my body-worn camera was hanging off my uniform shirt at an angle. After a quick examination, I saw that the clip was broken, and the back of the camera was separating from its casing. I was assigned to the patrol zone furthest from the station, so I opted to purchase electrical tape from the local convenience store to hold the camera together until the end of shift. It made more sense than having another officer cover my zone while taking the time to write the report for the broken equipment. The camera still functioned properly, and the tape did exactly what it was designed to do—hold shit together.

At the end of my shift, I returned to the station. I immediately advised my sergeant (a disciple of the two aforementioned haters) that my body-worn camera was broken, and I needed to write it up. I showed him what was wrong with the device and how I temporarily secured it. My sergeant advised not to worry about it. He said, "We will write it up on Monday morning."

"I am on vacation for the next two sets," I replied. "I won't be back to work for 10 days."

"Seriously, don't worry about it," he said. "I will try to remember to take care of it while you are out. If not, we will deal with it when you get back. Enjoy your time off."

Message received.

I was out of there before he could change his mind. My boss had less time on the job than me. He was nine badge numbers below mine and was known for his ass kissing, which explains his moving up the ranks so quickly. This guy's thoughts and opinions were never his own, and his alliances changed with the wind. He would praise a shitty cop and shit on his partner, if he felt it would keep him in good favor with the powers that be. When we were equal-ranking partners, he and I were chosen to serve as the proactive squad. It was during this time that he ran my name into the ground with our boss. In what I thought was casual conversation, this "partner" and soon-to-be sergeant made off-color comments about our boss. When I agreed with him, he turned around and told our boss what I thought of him. He was playing both sides. This kid was a dirty politician to the core. I was, by far, a better street cop, and he knew it. He just needed a way to get around me to secure his own career path.

It worked!

When I returned from vacation, we were back on the nightshift. I arrived just in time to put on my uniform and slide into rollcall with only seconds to spare.

"Sorry I'm late," I said. "I'm still in vacation mode."

Another officer chirped back, "Dude, you have been in vacation mode for the last year."

We all laughed, including myself. However, I did not find it funny. I was hurting, but everyone only saw a guy who was on a permanent vacation, or as we cynically called it, "retired on duty." That perception could not have been further from the truth.

This only exacerbated the situation.

When we broke from rollcall, I approached my boss and reminded him that I needed to write up my camera. He claimed to have no recollection of our conversation. It was clear he didn't do anything about it while I was away.

I later learned that I could not have been more wrong.

"Why do you need to report broken equipment," he asked, sounding a little odd and unnatural. I told him, again, what had happened to my body-worn camera on my last shift.

"Why did it take you 10 days to report this," he barked.

It was as if he did not hear a word I said or as though he was being coached and recording the conver ...

Oh shit!!

This fucking guy was going after me for the broken camera. He found a small chink in my armor and was going to exploit it. I was getting played, and he fucked me.

Again!

I was told to write a special incident report and detail the moments before and after the camera broke, including the time between me noticing the damage and the time I reported it. I saw where this was going, and I knew that they were going to do everything in their power to come after me. I had been there before, and I figured as long as I told the truth, the rest would play itself out.

Unfortunately, however, the truth was not good enough. Moreover, I did not know how the camera broke, nor did I know when it happened. This was unacceptable to them, and I was asked to take a guess and document it. Now, anyone who has ever conducted suspect or witness interviews knows that *this* is how you get someone to confess. Even if their "guess" is not accurate, it is how you close cases. I was not about to cater to his request like a skell being looked at for a Bodega robbery.

I was a rockstar cop reporting broken equipment.

Two weeks after submitting my report, I was called into the Internal Affairs office by the lieutenant in charge of the investigation. He handed me some standard IA paperwork that I was required to sign. I was being officially notified that I was under investigation for intentionally harming department-issued equipment and failing to report the damage. I was read my rights and told that I was going to be interviewed. With an overconfident tone and carefree laugh, I said, "Okay! I will see you then."

"Sit down and make yourself comfortable," the lieutenant advised. "The interview is about to begin."

So much for preparation.

Right then and there, I was forced to answer questions related to my special report. However, I was not allowed to use the report to refresh my recollection. Over the course of the next two hours, I was asked a slew of detailed questions that I answered from memory about an insignificant incident that took place a month prior.

It was a Friday afternoon. The interview with IA dragged out until the lieutenant finally had to go home. This guy was someone who I used to call "friend." I could not believe he was doing this to me. It was almost as if he had orders from above.

Hmmm ... perhaps this was the washer's tournament revenge.

On the way home from work that day, I had an epiphany. I recalled saying something during the interview that was 100 percent insignificant, but 100 percent untrue. I immediately called the lieutenant's work extension and left a voice message. I was sure not to call his cell phone, as I wanted full documentation of my disclosure and a time stamp on the message. I advised the lieutenant that during the interview I mentioned purchasing the tape at a mini mart. I wanted to correct my statement to reflect that I had purchased the tape at a 7-11. While there was a part of me that did not think this was a big deal, there was another part of me that was terrified. I knew I was doing the right thing, even though the significance of where I purchased the tape had absolutely no bearing on my story.

When I returned to work on Monday morning, I expected another interview with the IA lieutenant. Instead, we had a quick conversation. It was far from an actual interview. He acknowledged that he had received my voicemail message and requested I write another special report containing the information I shared.

Ugh ... not good.

It wasn't that I had anything to hide or that I provided untrue information. However, it was a change in my story. I knew that change, albeit small, was going to be a big deal.

I guess that is the price you pay for being honest.

CHAPTER SEVENTEEN
Distracted

A few weeks passed, and I had not heard anything more about the incident. I thought that was a good thing. Oftentimes, with the passage of time, situations get watered down and become less significant as other issues take precedent.

Not the case in this situation.

It was a Monday, and I was returning to the nightshift. I worked through the evening into Tuesday morning with my regular routine. I only did what was required of me and slept my way through most of the 12 hours. When I came back into the station, just prior to the shift change at 0600, the lieutenant's car was in the lot. He never showed up early.

This was not good.

"Follow me," the lieutenant said, greeting me at the door to the station. I quietly followed him into his office. There was a pit in my stomach. I was nauseous, fearing the worst.

As we sat facing each other, he handed me a few papers to sign. As I thumbed through them, I could not believe what I was reading. I was being charged with lying and providing false information. I had made what was the equivalent of a syntax error, and even though I immediately corrected it, I was being charged with an offense far greater.

This was an all-out assault on my job.

Police officers cannot be found guilty of lying and expect to keep their job, nor should they if what they are being charged with is, indeed, true. This is not only a moral dilemma, but also a legal one under the

Brady and Giglio court decisions. Officer integrity can become an affirmative defense for suspects in trial. If you cannot be considered truthful (at all costs), then your reports and court testimony are deemed useless. Moreover, an IA investigation like mine has to be filed with the state and is thereby discoverable by attorneys. That is to say, every case that I was a part of from that moment forward would trigger a "motion to dismiss" based on my history for "lack of candor." I would never be a credible witness again.

I was done!

As sad and disappointed as I was, I signed the papers with ease. In that moment, I knew everything was over—my career, my credibility, my social standing, my family, my life. In my heart I knew what was best and that was to permanently remove myself from the equation. If I was dead, if I killed myself, it would end this witch hunt and my department would not get the chance to fire me. Therefore, my family name would not be disgraced.

I was sad, not nearly ready to leave this earth, but I was resolute in my decision. It was the only way to "get past" this. I just hoped that my family would understand. I left the lieutenant's office with my head up. I went down to the locker room to change, and then I got into my car to "go home." Everyone offered cordial salutations on the way out, like we did after every shift.

But I said goodbye.

I actually felt bad because I knew what the days ahead would look like for the officers I left behind. I knew this would be something they could never have imagined. I knew they would look back on the past year and a half and suddenly see the signs. I knew they would have feelings of guilt. I also knew in time they would eventually move on. My only hope was that the next time someone was silently crying out for help, someone would hear it. It was a sad, yet realistic moment. It was all about control. I knew something they didn't know, and it was my choice. It was a feeling I never had before. It was very powerful. I felt very powerful. For the first time in a long time, I was the only one in control of my fate, no matter how ill-conceived it was. I wasn't scared. I was committed, and it felt good. I was only sad for my family and friends, knowing what was ahead of them. It was all very conscious.

Somewhere around 6:30 a.m., I drove away from the station, in the direction of my home. It was the same route I traveled every day. I generally did not pay attention to much, as is the case for anyone in a monotonous routine. However, that day was different. I had the windows rolled down. I felt the breeze, smelled the air, and I appreciated the familiarity of the scenery.

I was at peace, and I was calm, but my senses were at peak hyper-vigilance. I almost felt intoxicated. I was scared though … in fear of the pain I might feel when I discharged my weapon. Most of all, I was sad I did not have the chance to give my wife one last hug and kiss or leave my kids with one last snuggle. In that moment, I felt love in a way I hadn't in a long time.

I looked at the clock. It was 6:38 a.m. I was stopped at the red light on Route 571, at the intersection of Clarksville Road. While stopped, I decided I would pull into the police station of the neighboring town, just a half mile down the road, on the right. The plan was to pull into the parking lot, back into a space, make sure my lights were on, and shoot myself in the head. Just as Detective Sergeant O'Donnell had done. While it had been 20 years since his suicide, it felt like only yesterday. It was as though he left me a blueprint to follow. I was hoping that whoever found me would also hide the details of the investigation, so my kids would not have to learn about what had happened.

I was ready.

The timing of the red light felt like an eternity. I could not wait for it to turn green, so that I could go. Let's think about that for a second. I had a plan to kill myself in the next minute or two, and I was actually waiting for the green light before crossing through the intersection. That was my moment, my window, a space in time when I could be saved.

Fortunately, I was!

Just before the light turned green, my cell phone rang. The call was coming from my home number. When I answered the phone, my oldest son, Alex, said that he was up, out of bed, and getting ready for school.

"I just wanted to call and say good morning, in case you are running late and won't be home before I leave," he said.

Just then, the light turned green. I began to drive, and without even realizing it, I passed the location of the local police department where I was to end my life. By the time I hung up the phone, I was through that window in time and out of the darkest place I have ever been in my life.

My son saved my life.

Alex was 12 years old when this happened, and I have never talked to him about it. When he is mature enough and interested in reading this book, he will learn of this for the first time. In fact, there is only one other person I have told before writing about it in these pages. I never told my best friend, and I never told anyone at work. I never even told my wife. Now, I have told the world, and it is refreshing.

I have nothing to hide.

I don't believe in the "stigma" of suicidal ideation. If we don't share our truths, we only perpetuate the feelings of isolation endured by those who are struggling. Sometimes, things do seem so bad that one cannot see a proper path forward. What I do believe is that at a time when we are not thinking rationally, there is a small window of hope through which one can be reached. My son found mine.

I am reminded of the Kevin Hines story. If you haven't heard of him, let me pull a paragraph from the website—www.kevinhinesstory.com. It reads: "Kevin Hines is a storyteller. He is a bestselling author, global public speaker, and award-winning documentary filmmaker. In the year 2000, Kevin attempted to take his life by jumping off the Golden Gate Bridge. Many factors contributed to his miraculous survival, including a sea lion which kept him afloat until the Coast Guard arrived. Kevin now travels the world sharing his story of hope, healing, and recovery while teaching people of all ages the art of wellness and the ability to survive pain with true resilience."

In his own words, Kevin explains that if one person had stopped to talk to him at any point, from the time he left his house to the time he jumped, he would have told them everything. He would have never jumped. So, if you see that someone is struggling, be the one to climb through the window, like my son climbed through mine, you may just save their life.

I love you, Alex, with all my heart. If not for you on that day and in that moment, someone else would be telling my story and this book would end with this chapter. I am grateful I am still here to tell my story, and there are many more chapters to come.

CHAPTER EIGHTEEN
Poker Face

When I arrived home that morning, my head was foggy. I was emotionally distant. Frankly, I was exhausted. While this type of fatigue is normal following a nightshift, this morning was different.

I was not supposed to be there.

I was not supposed to make it home that day. I was supposed to be the blank page at the end of a book—this book. I was supposed to be dead. I found myself in the comfort of my own home, surrounded by my wife and children, embraced with love, and I knew that everything was going to be okay. For the first time, I realized I was not *just* a cop. I was a husband and a dad and no one, not even the Internal Affairs lieutenant, could take that away from me.

Later that morning, after everyone left the house for the day, I laid in bed, feeling at peace for the first time in a long time. I struggled to fall asleep, not because my brain was hyperactive, as it usually was, but because I wanted to enjoy being awake, conscious of each breath, each heartbeat. I wanted to embrace being alive.

I did not want to feel dead.

I eventually drifted off to sleep, waking up in the early afternoon. The kids came home from school. The wife returned from work, and life went on as usual. I lived alone with this awful secret.

Until now.

That secret and subsequent isolation took its toll on me and came back to haunt me later. I felt as though I had cheated on my family, my friends, and my coworkers. I felt as though my secret was somehow visible to others, and there would always be a visible question mark hanging over people's heads when they interacted with me.

Did they know I was hiding something?

If so, why didn't they ask me about it? And if they didn't ask, did that mean they did not care? Were they too scared to learn the truth? My secret caused me shame, embarrassment, isolation, inspiration, strength, and power all at the same time. It was the strangest dichotomy of emotions.

Not long after I signed the Internal Affairs' paperwork, I received the findings of the full investigation, along with the suggested repercussions for my actions. The charges of misuse of department-issued equipment that caused significant damage, failure to report that damage, and lack of candor during the investigation would all be sustained. While I was not surprised, it was still a hard punch to the gut because the facts of the case had been manipulated to fit an agenda versus to determine an outcome. They were not wrong, but they were not right either.

I received a 16-day suspension.

It was an outrageous amount of time, not to mention inconsistent with the charges. Nevertheless, I was not going to give them the satisfaction of an appeal. That would only drag me further through the proverbial mud and make this case visible to others. If I accepted the punishment, the case was closed. No one who knew about the case, including the IA lieutenant, could discuss it. That confidentiality allowed me to tell my side of the story without a response from those involved. This story was mine to tell.

My 16-day suspension proved to have a significant impact on the work schedule for my patrol squad, not to mention on my pay. Those 16 days totaled $9,000 in lost pay, nearly an entire month's salary. The patrol lieutenant responsible for the schedule met with me privately. In confidence, he told me he was disgusted with how I was treated and was admonished for even saying so to the other lieutenants and the chief. The patrol lieutenant asked me how I wanted to serve the suspension.

"Do you want to take the next 16 shifts off or would you like to take one shift per week, which would impact two shifts per pay period?"

He was willing to work with me, giving me control of how best to serve my time. I could take the hit all at once, or I could spread it over several months. If I took the 16 suspension days consecutively, I would have to surrender my badge, police ID, and service weapon. I would also have to add that time to the end of my career, and it would be disclosed on public record. I chose to take the extended option—one to two days per pay cycle. I worked with the patrol lieutenant to limit the impact of the patrol schedule, but I also took the days I knew would best serve my personal schedule. Looking back, I turned an unfortunate situation around to serve me and my family. After all, I owed it to my wife and children. What's more, I owed it to myself because I came really close to ending it all. I was literally seconds away from never spending time with them again.

Every one of my scheduled suspension days was used to do something special as a family. Some days, it was as simple as going out for ice cream or on a bike ride. We made sure we took full advantage of the gift we were given to be together, never dwelling on the implications of lost wages. My wife was so supportive through this process. Quite frankly, she was even more angry about the situation than I was. The support she showed me was more important than she will ever know. It gave me confidence, knowing that no matter what happened, we would get through it together.

Days and weeks went by and the suspension days, or "super days" as we referred to them at work, became a bit of a running joke. The rumors as to why I was suspended became more and more entertaining by the minute. While everyone knew the issue stemmed from a broken, body-worn camera, no one had any other information. I got wind of some of the stories going around. Most of the stories were benign, like the seatbelt ripped the camera off my shirt when I was exiting the car. Other stories were more scandalous. For example, one story alluded to me intentionally breaking the camera after realizing it was running when I was speaking negatively about the chief. My favorite rumor was that I had sex with a township employee while on nightshift, and the camera inadvertently activated during "the act," and the incident was recorded. I won't name the person I was suspected of engaging with sexually because she still lives in and works for the township, but I will say I was utterly offended by the insinuation that I did not have better taste in women.

Seriously, guys?!

If I were to ever cheat on my wife, which I never have and never will, it would not have been with that. The Gene Simmons look is not my jam. Please, if you are going to accuse me of infidelity, at least do not disrespect my standards.

With all the rumors floating around, I remained silent. Just to get a laugh, I waited to see how far they would go. It was incredibly entertaining to watch the stress-o-meter rise from the powers that be because they were not able to respond to the rumors and accusations about them targeting me. They also lost the respect of many officers because there was no good reason for such a significant punishment. As time passed, I began to reveal the facts of the story, and they were so mild that folks didn't believe me.

The punishment did not fit the proverbial crime.

The conversation became so publicly concerning within the agency that the chief, himself, (the former sergeant who tried destroying my career after my wife beat him in a backyard washers tournament), felt he had to personally address it with me. So, he called me down to his office, but not before publicly announcing that I was "not in trouble." The chief put up a front, saying something about "having questions about a project he was working on." I guess he did not want any more rumors to spread.

When we got to his office, the chief addressed the entire situation from start to finish. I was smart enough to not play along. I did not respond to anything he said or covertly asked. The case was closed and could not be reopened, unless I said something that was not consistent with my original statement. I could tell he was uncomfortable with my silence. It almost felt as though he needed to fill the empty space, like a suspect would during a criminal interview. I had turned the dynamic of the conversation on him.

He told me that *he* was the one to recommend the excessive suspension (his words) in hopes I would appeal. He was looking for the fight and wanted the entire situation exposed. To this day, I believe he wanted to fire me, but needed to have a "public stoning" to do so. If I had not accepted the suggested suspension and went on to appeal it, I would have forfeited the initial suggestion of the 16 days, and I would have opened myself up to being fired. By accepting the 16 days, the case was closed and could never be reopened. The chief tried backing me into a corner with the threat of financial hardship.

Check.

However, since my family is financially secure, I was able to end the game and control the narrative.

Checkmate.

What a fucking loser!

At this point in my life, I actually feel bad for the guy. I can't imagine going through life with such a profound feeling of insecurity that I would hold onto such a grudge against a fellow officer, waiting 10 years to exact my revenge in such a vicious and evil way.

In the grand scheme of things, the $9,000 was not a significant loss, and I grew to appreciate the unexpected vacation time with my family. And, as it turned out, my strength in the face of adversity also proved inspirational for many of my brothers and sisters on the job. I had been dragged into the depths of darkness by the department administration, to the point where I saw suicide as my only option. Fortunately, for me, I was saved by the sound of my child's voice, and I saw the light that shined in the eyes of my family. I was finally able to move forward through these challenging waters to a place where love overcomes evil.

Love always wins.

CHAPTER NINETEEN
Punching Out

In the summer of 2019, I toyed with the idea of retiring at the end of the year. It would mark 20 years and one month of service, making me eligible for the New Jersey Special Service Retirement Program. In the state of New Jersey, a full-service retirement through the Police and Fire Retirement System (PFRS) was 25 years of service, with no age limit. This entitled you to a pension worth 65 percent of your base salary, plus full medical benefits for you and your family until your eligibility for Medicare. A special service retirement entitles you to a pension of 50 percent of your salary and no health benefits. Despite all the shortcomings of the town I worked for, our contract had a clause that all police officers who completed 20 years of service were eligible for lifetime benefits. So, to leave with 20 years instead of 25, all I was losing was approximately $12,000 a year from my pension, not to mention the stress of a job I no longer needed or wanted.

For nearly the last two years at work, I was only going through the motions. In my heart, I still wanted to be in a position to help others, but I was so broken, I could not even help myself. I did not have the right vocabulary to express all that was happening to me. However, in hindsight, I was very aware that it was time to go. While I was exposed to a lot of trauma over the years in EMS and police work, and it contributed to my declining mental and physical health, it was the stress of department and agency politics (organizational trauma) that put me over the edge. I was more worried about being stabbed in the back inside the police station than shot in the face outside of it. I felt safer around criminals and thugs than I did my own colleagues and bosses.

I discussed my retirement with my wife. She was in full support of it. She saw the toll the stress was taking on me, and she knew it was not sustainable. Stephanie had also been contemplating her own professional future. At the time, she did not see much opportunity for growth in the position she held. She was the director of marketing for a large consumer packaged goods company, and the chain of command she reported up through was stable. There was not likely to be any movement in the near future. Moreover, she was burned out from the corporate world.

While a master at her craft, my wife had moved away from the art of marketing and into personnel management and Wall Street reporting, which was not exciting for her. She yearned for the opportunity to get back to her passion and even dreamed of leaving corporate life behind and starting her own business as a marketing consultant. Stephanie knew that if I retired and was able to be the primary parent at home, she could leave her job and transition into a new chapter of her career.

Over the next few months, we met with the State Division of Pensions, our financial advisors, and accountant. By the end of August, I filed for retirement and was approved by the State Pension Board. The department was notified electronically, and word spread quickly. After communicating my intentions to the town, I was also approved for my retirement medical benefits.

I was ready to go.

There was a noticeable change in the way I was treated. Some of the younger guys wrote me off, and some tried to tap into my knowledge and experience before I left. The bosses seemed to be taken aback by my decision and stayed clear of me at all costs. I thought it was odd, until one of them asked me the million-dollar question, "Who are you going to sue on the way out?"

"I guess you will have to wait and see," I replied with a chuckle. I never planned on suing anyone, though I probably could have. That sue-happy mentality was just not me. I can't deny it though; it was nice to see them squirm.

∽

Throughout 2019, I experienced increasing pain in my right shoulder. There was also a decrease in strength and movement. On August 30th, I was told I needed surgery to repair a torn biceps tendon. Unfortunately, it was not a work-related injury, so I had to either wait until after my retirement date to have it repaired or use sick time to have the procedure done. The good news was I had more than enough sick time to take me to the end of the year and still get a full terminal leave check for my unused time. I made the tough decision to have my shoulder repaired on September 10, 2019. The recovery process took four months, which would take me to the end of the year. My last day of work was nightshift on Sunday, September 8, 2019.

I could not believe it.

As ready as I was to go, I was not prepared. After 20 years of wearing the uniform, that was the last time I put it on. For the first time in a long time, I arrived at work early. I took it all in. My wife and kids came to the station, and we took a ton of pictures. I gave them one final tour. They sat in my police car one last time, playing with the lights and siren, and just before the start of my shift, they gave me one final salute before they left for home. I sat in on my final rollcall, and at 0200 hours on September 9, 2019, I answered my final calls for service. And just like that, I signed off for the last time.

It was a bittersweet moment when I returned to the locker room to change into my civilian clothes. I was the only one there, and I felt as lonely as I did on my first day on the job, 20 years prior. I cleaned out my locker, left the department-issued equipment, and walked out with a box of personal items and a heart full of memories. It was the last time I drove away from the station as an East Windsor police officer.

I returned to the station for a small retirement ceremony on December 31, 2019. There were four of us leaving that day, although not everyone showed up. My friend, Joe, was leaving after 25 years of service, all with East Windsor. The Internal Affairs lieutenant was leaving with 25 years of service—22 of which were with East Windsor. And the patrol lieutenant, who did not show up to the ceremony, was leaving with 25 years of service—24 of which were with East Windsor. He was so disenfranchised because of the way he was treated by the chief and by what had happened to me, he quietly walked out of the station on the Friday before the ceremony and never looked back.

While I, too, harbored hostility for both the agency and the chief, I allowed myself to experience the retirement ceremony as if it were a genuine, heartfelt sendoff. I had many great years serving the community where I was born and raised, and I truly felt like I had given everything I had and was allowed to give.

I showed up to that last event for me and no one else.

The chief opened up the ceremony with some introductory remarks about the agency and welcomed all those in attendance. I was blessed to be sharing the experience with my wife, my children, and my best friend,

Adam, who is a major with the Maryland State Police. Also in attendance were former colleagues, current colleagues, family members of the other retiring officers, and some other community notables.

Following the chief's speech, I was called up to the podium. The chief recapped my career aloud to the audience. While I was never promoted, I had an incredible experience, and I appreciated hearing some of it read back to me in this format. I will say, though, it felt a bit like a professional eulogy.

It must have been my mindset at the time.

I was excited to be in a position that would allow me to create a new chapter in my life's story, but I was sad to be leaving the job. It felt like a funeral for my policing career. Looking back, it was even more than that. It was the beginning of my next downward spiral.

I really enjoyed listening to the chief open up about me. Honestly, it was the first time I ever heard him say anything nice. I'm not sure if I was oddly happy to finally have some validation from him or if it was pure spite because he was forced to publicly praise me, and I was hoping it was burning him up inside. Either way, I embraced it. After his remarks, I had an opportunity to say a few words. I did not have anything prepared, so I kept it to a short, obligatory thank you to all in attendance. I expressed my sincerest appreciation for the honor to serve my hometown community for so many years. My emotions took over, and I began to cry. I was fully entering a state of loss, and in that moment, I began to mourn my career.

Reality was setting in.

The chief presented me with a shiny, mahogany plaque. Affixed to it were my original chest badge, hat badge, a few decorative pins, and my uniform name tag. On the bottom, there was a brass nameplate noting my years of service. I graciously received the plaque and shook the chief's hand and said, "Thank you."

I then hugged my colleagues and suddenly, I felt like I mattered. I felt like my career mattered. My heart was full. Before I was able to walk back to my seat, I was told there was one more presentation to be made. My best friend, Adam, approached the podium and gave me a proclamation signed by, and on behalf of, the colonel of the Maryland State Police. It was in recognition of my service to the Maryland State Police and the citizens of Maryland for my work with the Police Unity Tour, honoring Adam's academy roommate since his line of duty death in 2011. This will always be one of my most prized possessions, along with the plaque and my framed accommodations that now hang on my office wall.

The "I Love Me" wall!

The three other retirees were then called up, one at a time, and all were presented with their plaque. When the patrol lieutenant's name was called, his bio was shared, and he was honored, even though he wasn't in attendance. All things considered … I thought it was a classy move. I am just sorry he was not there to see how much he was appreciated by the other members of the agency. The ceremony was followed by a small reception with a cake, great storytelling, and some tearful goodbyes. I walked up the stairs to the main floor and through the building one more time as an active-duty police officer. Then, with my wife holding my hand and my other arm around my children, I walked out of the back door for the final time—my head held high. I embraced the moment but could not believe it. There was a part of me that was excited to rediscover myself in this next chapter. Another part of me wanted it all back.

It was so surreal.

We got into the car. I paused for a brief moment, and then we drove away. As I looked into the rearview mirror, the police station got smaller and smaller. It was a visual metaphor of my law enforcement career.

CHAPTER TWENTY
From Taps to Amazing Grace

Growing up in East Windsor, I had many close friends. However, as I mentioned earlier, my best friend was Adam. When I use the term "best friend," what I mean to say is that Adam is family. I call his dad on Father's Day. I call his mom on Mother's Day. His daughter has my heart, and his son is my godson.

Yes, I am the Jewish godfather to a Christian kid.

It works for us because it is less about religion and all about the significance of our relationship. I love Adam's kids as if they were my own. Adam and I share a passion for police work. We both wanted to follow in his father's footsteps. His dad, Jack, was a 25-year police officer in the town we grew up in. After my first summer as a Special Police Officer in Seaside Park in 1998, Adam joined me there for the summer of 1999. I had already been to the police academy and was looking for a full-time position. He was expecting to go to the academy after the summer was over and was also applying to different agencies around the country. I wound up in East Windsor, and Adam was selected by the Maryland State Police, a position he was proud to accept. He went through the academy in early 2000. Adam's roommate was a guy named Shaft Hunter. The two became fast friends, building a relationship that lasted well into their careers. By all accounts, Shaft was a great friend of mine, too. I was fortunate to get to know and love him.

Years later, in the early morning hours of May 21, 2011, I got the call that no law enforcement officer wants to get, but in the back of our mind is always anticipating. It was 0300 when the phone rang. The caller ID on my phone read Adam's number.

Not good.

You may recall; I have a rule with friends and family. They can call me anytime of the day or night, and I will pick up the phone.

It is more of a promise, really.

If you need me, I will be there. If you are drunk, I will still be there, but best be sure I will kick your ass when you sober up. True to my promise, I picked up the phone in the middle of that horrific night. Before I could get a word out, I heard frantic crying. It was Adam. He told me something had happened to Shaft.

"He was in a crash," he cried. "He's gone."

It took me a minute to process the words, but as the news sunk in, I, too, was stricken with emotion, and quickly became inconsolable. Trooper First Class Shaft Sidney Hunter was a decorated captain in the United States Marine Corps and a storied member of the Maryland State Police's K-9 unit. Shaft was on-duty when he engaged in a vehicle pursuit on Route 95 South in Howard County Maryland. The suspect (wanted for murder) was on a motorcycle. The speeds of the pursuit went well into the triple digits, as both Shaft and the suspect approached the Laurel Rest Stop, a popular spot for over-the-road truckers. It is the last stop on Route 95 before Washington, DC. Because the trucks at this location quickly fill up the parking lot, it is not uncommon for many of them to park illegally on the shoulder of the roadway leading to and from the rest stop entrance and exit.

This night was no different.

The suspect proceeded south, and Shaft's car would disappear. His radio transmissions went unanswered. His computer was no longer sending a signal. Upon the arrival of another trooper responding as a back-up officer, the worst possible scenario was discovered. Trooper First Class Shaft Hunter struck one of the illegally parked trucks from behind. It protruded out into the lane of travel, and it did not have any lights on. Shaft's patrol vehicle hit the left half of the ICC bar on the trailer, the horizontal piece of steel that prevents vehicles from getting underneath the truck. Shaft's patrol vehicle all but disintegrated. As the investigation ensued, Adam was notified, not just as a close friend and colleague but as a supervisor. I will never forget that night or that call.

It will live with me forever.

Once again, not only did I feel the loss and grief for both Adam and me, but I also felt a sense of helplessness for not being there, in that moment, to support him. I needed a way to be a constructive part of the healing, the ability to comfort or serve others as a way to console my own emotions. Speaking of emotions, the days following Shaft's death were a strange combination of sadness, heartbreak, storytelling, and bonding with friends and family—blood and Blue. It was a brief, uncomfortable void of time between death and a funeral, where time stood still. Funerals are a milestone in the grieving process that no one is quite ready for, yet most cannot wait for them to come.

At that point in my career, I had been to my share of police funerals. They are all personal because when a police officer is killed in the line of duty, it is not just another loss. The family loses a loved one. The department loses a valuable member of the team. The community loses one of its protectors, and a nation loses one of its steadfast patriots. Then, as a police officer attending the funeral of a fallen brother or sister, you lose a piece of yourself. You recognize your own vulnerabilities. You consider your own mortality, and you wonder if you are next, and if not you … then who?

You imagine elaborate arrangements of flowers with your name on them. You picture your medals displayed on the stand. You envision your family weeping, and you see yourself inside of the wooden box. Law enforcement officers work in a world where the next traffic stop can be their last. The next call for service can be their last. What is worse, they can be ambushed when sitting in their patrol car or in standing line at a coffee shop simply because they wear the uniform. They can also be like Shaft, one-third of the yearly line-of-duty deaths, killed in a vehicle crash. It is a dangerous job. We know that, so when faced with the reality of our own mortality, shit gets real—real fast.

As an officer, I have grown with each funeral experience. However, Shaft's was different. It hurt more. Shaft was my friend. He was a brother to my brother. He was more like family. I knew his family. I knew the three moms to his five children.

Yes! You read that right.

I know his brothers. I know his parents, and I know his kids. The youngest, at the time of his death, was only one year old. When I looked at his kids, I saw my own.

That was devastating to me.

I remember being at Adam's house the morning of the funeral. The house was quiet, and the air was heavy. We were preparing for the day, getting dressed in our Class-A uniforms. Our shirts, pants and dress blouses were perfectly pressed. Our leather gear was positioned just right, and our parade shoes were perfectly polished. Our gloves were the whitest white. Our brass glistened in the sunshine, and our covers were perfectly square. We captured this moment in our respective uniforms with a set of pictures I cherish to this day. If you look close enough, you can see Shaft in the sun's rays above us.

We arrived at the church in Adam's flawlessly detailed troop car, parking amongst a sea of police vehicles from as far north as Vermont, as far south as Florida, and as far west as California. There were also several military vehicles present in support of Shaft's service in the United States Marine Corps. As we approached the church entrance, we walked past law enforcement officers from almost every state, including a group of Maryland State Troopers and the Maryland State Police command staff. We made our way up to the front of the sanctuary and greeted the extended Hunter family, expressing our condolences. It was such a formal and surreal experience. I felt so disconnected from the moment. I cannot even begin to imagine how Shaft's family felt.

The service was heartfelt and genuine, but to be honest, I don't remember it well. My clearest memory is seeing Adam crying as the service was ending. That broke my heart and comforted me at the same time. It was the first time I had seen a friend cry, and it gave me permission to do the same. As a cop, it was the first time I recognized it was okay to show emotion, especially while in uniform. Since I took my oath, it was the first time I gave myself permission to be vulnerable. Moreover, it was the first time I cried in years. Through all my sadness and grief, it felt good. I felt human for the first time in a long time, and in the midst of a fellow officer's death, I felt so alive.

Like most funerals for fallen uniformed officers, the bugle called to order the message of Taps, the musical language for "Day is Done." After the final note, we were ordered to mark a moment of silence. As we reflected in our grief, the empty space was soon filled with the

175

heart-wrenching cry of the bagpipes, performing Amazing Grace. Each note that was played had enough might to lift the spirit from the body of the deceased and forever stick in the hearts of those present. While most police officers will survive their career and make it through to retirement, we will suffer the death of our soul a thousand times over. With every call for service, fatal crash, death of a child, battered spouse and each tragedy we witness, we leave a piece of ourselves behind. Each time that happens, we mourn a piece of our soul. This hardens us in such a way that we forget how to show emotion.

We forget how to love.

We forget how to cry.

We forget that we, too, are human.

Shaft's death and funeral came days after National Police Week in 2011. Having just returned home from the events in Washington, DC, it did not take long to figure out the best way for me to honor my friend. That summer, I bought a new road bike and registered for the 2012 Police Unity Tour ride in the fall. I began my training, and within a few weeks, I was riding up to 25 miles per day—100 miles per week. It would be through the Police Unity Tour's mission that I would honor the fallen and find healing in the process.

CHAPTER TWENTY-ONE
The Wind at My Back

As a police officer, there are many memorable moments in my career, exciting calls, and important assignments I have undertaken that made me feel accomplished. However, there is nothing more special and meaningful than my involvement with the Police Unity Tour. The primary purpose of this organization, as it reads on their website, "is to raise awareness of law enforcement officers who have died in the line of duty." The secondary purpose "is to raise funds for the National Law Enforcement Officers Memorial." Since its inception in 1997, they have raised more than $33 million dollars with the help of more than 2,600 members nationwide.

In 2012, I was the first person from my agency to ever participate in this event. When I told people I registered, the reactions were mixed. There were those who were generally supportive and thought it would be a cool experience. There were, of course, the usual naysayers who thought it was stupid. Some did not believe I had what it took to ride 300 miles in just four days on a small seat, skinny tires, and no motor. Then there was department leadership, more concerned with liability, time off, and what it would mean to represent the agency without their personal supervision.

Leadership was the biggest hurdle to get over.

As I had come to expect, their response was a poor representation of true leadership. When leaders don't trust their people, they fail to inspire trust for and in themselves. Not only that, but they fail to motivate and strengthen people's work ethic and agency loyalty. I literally had to write a letter to the chief requesting permission to put an agency patch on my bike jersey. I was told that I was not allowed to use the department name in any other way. Everything else had to go through the union. What is important to understand here is that our agency did not participate in anything outside of our jurisdiction. I was breaking the mold.

I was always breaking the mold, and they hated me for it.

Fundraising quickly got underway. I could not believe how generous folks were and how genuinely excited most people were to support this cause. At the time, each rider was required to raise $1,650. Today, they are required to raise $1,950. Donations came from local, small businesses, larger corporations, the local Police Benevolent Association (PBA), friends, family and the East Windsor Education Association, led by my friend and mentor Ellen. Through the PRIDE grant program, the EWEA has contributed $1,000 every year for the last 10 years and will continue to do so for as long as we ride.

That first year as a single rider, I raised almost $5,000. Over the course of 12 years, I have raised nearly $75,000. For the first several years, I was the only member of my agency to participate. I joined forces with another local department, so I would not have to ride alone. As the years moved forward, I was able to get a handful of other officers involved.

After months of training and attending monthly meetings, the day arrived—May 9, 2012. We were ready to roll. Day one was a 60-mile ride from Florham Park, New Jersey to Edison, New Jersey. We rode on highways and byways, but the most exciting segments were down the main streets of several towns along the way. There were families and supporters lining the sidewalks. Blue Line flags were everywhere, and police were controlling traffic at every intersection. There were fire trucks with extended ladders strung with American flags that hung over the street for us to ride underneath. I had not felt that inspired since September 12, 2001.

Day two was a 100+ miles from Edison to Wilmington, Delaware. Day three was another 100 miles from Wilmington to Annapolis, Maryland. Day four was a 40-mile ride from Annapolis to the National Law Enforcement Officers Memorial in Washington, DC.

While the ride was long and tiring, the weather was mixed and intermittent. Nourishment consisted primarily of Gatorade and Smucker's Uncrustables. The emotional reward came when we rode through the walls of the memorial. There were 25,000 supporters cheering us on. There is no way to accurately describe the feelings I had in that moment, both physical and emotional. The tension in my back was not from poor riding form. It was from carrying the weight of my brothers and sisters whose names are etched into that wall. The pain on my bottom was not from sitting on a skinny seat for 300 miles. It was from the motivational "kick in the ass" I got, the fuel I used to keep pedaling. The tightness in my chest was not because I was out of breath. It was the love I felt from those who we hold in our heart, as we remember their life and selfless service.

The National Law Enforcement Officers Memorial was erected in 1991, beginning with the names of 12,000 law enforcement officers killed in the line of duty. It is hallowed ground. While there are no police officers buried there, the sacrifice of thousands will live on for eternity in that place. Currently, there are more than 23,000 names etched into the marble panels that make up the wall. The wall was constructed in such a way that it would allow for 100 years before needing more space to add names. Sadly, in 2021, just 30 years later, the marble panels were nearly filled, and the memorial had to be expanded. With an average of 160 law enforcement officers killed in the line of duty every year, it's no wonder.

And that number continues to rise.

At one time, vehicular crashes were the leading cause of officer fatalities. With the rise in violent crime and a shift in political and social norms, we are seeing felonious attacks against law enforcement outnumber vehicle crashes. In 2022, more than 350 officers were shot in the line of duty, 64 of which were fatal.

That same year, there were 230 fallen. Over the course of the last five years, we have lost 1,689–2,525 in the last 10 years. Every 48 hours, down from 58 hours in recent years, a peace officer is killed protecting our families and communities. Each year, there are over 68,000 assaults (up 10,000 per year since 2020) and more than 7,000 career-ending injuries (up 20%) in law enforcement.

To top it off, there are approximately 180 (known) suicides of active-duty officers every year. Additionally, there is an increase in K9 officers being killed in service, mostly by gunfire, an average of 10 per year.

The Memorial is guarded by four bronzed lions—two male and two female. Each watches over a pair of lion cubs on the opposing wall. The Memorial website reads, "... the statues symbolize the protective role of our law enforcement officers and convey the strength, courage, and valor that are the hallmarks of those who serve."

Beneath each adult lion is a quotation:

"It is not how these officers died that made them heroes,
it is how they lived."
—Vivian Eney Cross, Survivor

"In valor there is hope."
—Tacitus

"The wicked flee when no man pursueth,
but the righteous are as bold as a lion."
—Proverbs 28:1

"Carved on these walls is the story of America, of a continuing quest to
preserve both democracy and decency, and to protect a national treasure
that we call the American dream."
—President George H. W. Bush

Across the street from the Memorial is the National Law Enforcement Museum. It was created in 2018 to tell the story of American law enforcement. The museum houses several interactive exhibits, featuring many of our nation's notorious cases and displaying incredible acts of heroism. It also features a Hall of Remembrance that, like the National Memorial, is completely funded by the money raised by the Police Unity Tour. I could not be prouder to be a small part of this important mission that, as of May 12, 2023, has raised more than $36 million. My experience with the Police Unity Tour has introduced me to many great friendships. I have expanded my personal and professional network far beyond anything I could have ever imagined. The officers I ride with range from my old department to local, county, state, and national partners from across the country. Some are even as far away as Canada, London, Israel, and Australia. I have even had the great honor of befriending Craig Floyd the founding CEO of the Memorial Fund.

Craig and I met during my first ride in 2012. We became acquainted while riding next to each other on the first leg of the journey. We stayed in touch over the years, even into his retirement from the Memorial Fund in 2018. Craig is now the founding CEO of an organization called Citizens Behind the Badge. This group was founded to combat the rise of the "Defund the Police" movement and the political hate speech spawned against police officers during the civil unrest from 2020 to 2021. In early 2022, I was honored with an invite to become a member of the Law Enforcement Advisory Council for the organization. Craig, himself, invited me to help guide and support the mission. The vision of Citizens Behind the Badge is *"to become the leading voice of the American people in support of the men and women in law enforcement."* Our mission is *"to put an end to the misguided and disastrous movement to 'defund the police' and to ensure that our law enforcement professionals receive the support and resources needed to keep America safe."*

In its first fiscal year, Citizens Behind the Badge reached more than six million people from sea to shining sea, receiving donations from more than 100,000 people. There are more than 40,000 signed declarations of support, which we will be using to lobby members of congress for the enactment of pro-police legislation.

Again, like my involvement with the Police Unity Tour, it is truly an honor to be a small part of the change that helps support our law enforcement officers. When I reflect on the tragic and heartbreaking loss of my friend, Trooper First Class Shaft Sidney Hunter, I no longer feel the pain of grief, the weight of sadness and the void he left in our lives. Instead, I feel passion, drive, and meaning when honoring his memory and the memories of so many police officers we have buried along the way.

To my brothers and sisters who have paid the ultimate price while serving your respective communities, the courage and bravery you have shown is well represented in the bronzed lions that watch over you. You and your legacies will live on forever with every pedal stroke of my bike and every story shared. You and your service will never be forgotten!

CHAPTER TWENTY-TWO
Where the Road Ends

J anuary 1, 2020 was not like any other New Year's Day. For me, it was a New Life Day. It was a new beginning, complete with new titles, new definitions, and new purpose. My new identity was that of a retired law enforcement officer. I felt like I was on a permanent vacation, and as the winter break came to an end, I quickly fell into a new routine:

0600: Wake up

0700: Get the kids and wife off to school and work

0800: Work out

0900-1500: Do whatever the hell I want

1530: Welcome the kids home and help them with their homework

1800: The wife comes home

1900: Dinner

2100: Nighttime routine

I became the family taxi driver for baseball practice. I was at every school event, and in between, I lunched with other retired cops. I was available for all of the important parts of life, and I never wanted that feeling to end. However, toward the end of February, I started feeling something different, a sensation I did not recognize but felt oddly familiar. The retirement euphoria was waning, and feelings of isolation, loneliness, and lack of purpose were starting to fill in the blanks. News reports were consumed with talk of a new, global virus, insurrection, and political transition. While I considered my next professional move, all I really wanted to do was to go back to being a cop. It was not only what I knew, it was what I knew best. It was where I felt most at peace, even in the midst of chaos.

I was in complete regret of my decision to retire.

My thoughts turned sour. My vision narrowed, and everything blurred. The world seemed to be closing in around me. I was having night terrors, terrible dreams of calls for service gone bad. I heard the screams of children I could not save. I felt the heat of a fire I could not extinguish. I saw evil with such vividness that I could not dismiss it as fiction. I tasted blood and smelled rotting flesh. I felt death's cold touch because I could no longer understand and feel life.

My wife, Stephanie, left her corporate job in early March to start her own consulting business. She worked hard and developed an incredible business plan. Her business took off. She was an instant success. I was so proud of her, as she is one of *the* smartest humans I know. She has an Emotional Intelligence (EQ) that matches her Intelligence Quotient (IQ).

I will admit, however, I was quite jealous that Stephanie was able to pivot so seamlessly. Meanwhile, I was drowning. As my wife was redesigning her professional future, I established my own consulting company in hopes of using my law enforcement knowledge and background to help others. At first, I planned to teach and consult companies on active shooter response.

Boom! Insert COVID-19.

I failed.

Then came a change in the cannabis laws in New Jersey. I saw an opening for use-and-abuse education regarding workplace impairment. Much to my surprise, no one gave a shit.

Boom! I failed again.

Then I looked into using my training and experience as a drug recognition expert, supporting defense attorneys with client cases, something I vowed never to do. Unfortunately, cops were no longer making traffic stops or arrests.

Boom! I failed for a third time.

I tried to dig into my bag of professional experience, and at every turn, I failed. I was becoming resentful, angry, and depressed. I was spiraling downward—out of control. Like Maverick and Goose in Top Gun, I had flown through everyone else's jet wash. My engines were shutting down, and I was in a flat spin headed out to sea. My relationship with my wife was falling apart. I was continually yelling at my kids. I was isolating myself from my friends, and I felt like hope was out of reach. While my heart was still beating and my lungs were actively exchanging oxygen and carbon dioxide, my soul was quickly dying. My birthday falls in the middle of May, and while I love the opportunity to celebrate life, 2020's birthday celebration was bittersweet. As someone who has a propensity to see the glass half empty, turning 45 was sobering.

I struggled to see my future.

A few days after my birthday, our national landscape turned upside down and inside out. A Minneapolis police officer had a fatal encounter with an African-American man who was a known player in the drug trade, not to mention a local thief. While the suspect was complicit in his own demise, I condemn (in the strongest terms) the lack of empathy and professionalism the officer showed leading to the suspect's death.

As this incident sparked division and riots throughout our country and beyond, I fell deeper and deeper into my own dark hole. The county task force I was once a part of was activated and deployed to support the local riots in Trenton, New Jersey. I listened to the police radio traffic on my scanner. I could hear (in real-time) my friends getting attacked. I looked for a way to get involved. I volunteered to work at an aid station, sit in the comms center or throw on an old uniform and engage in the fight.

Anything.

As the violence and angst ensued, I learned that my home was on a potential Antifa/BLM hit list. If that wasn't bad enough, my wife's cousin wrote a public message on social media, calling for the "demise of cops." His side of the family all "liked" and supported his hateful message. I confronted him in a phone conversation, and he actually told me that he wished me dead and that he would be willing to kill me himself.

My world was collapsing around me.

I could not sleep.

I was up all night, conducting perimeter checks of my home.

I was losing my mind.

I spent my days visiting with my brothers and sisters who were still active-duty police officers, trying to support them in any way I could, but *I* was the one who was going crazy.

I had one friend who seemed to have it worse. He was spiralling faster than me. I will call him Danny. Danny was a detective sergeant at the time, serving with the Trenton City Police Department. He had been struggling with marital issues and his wife's betrayal for eight months or so, which he was very public about on social media. I talked to him about it often, but he continually assured me that he was just venting and that he was fine. He even joked about it. "When I stop venting," he said. "Then you should be concerned."

Danny was born and raised in the Trenton area. He was a department legacy. His father was one of the city's most infamous detectives. Danny was a jokester, known for his relentless pranks. He was, by all accounts, an incredible detective with unprecedented success in the street crimes unit. He was well respected by his peers, his supervisors, and subordinates. He also had a commanding presence, the ability to storm into any administrator's office and offer up his opinion on anything, whether it was solicited or not. Most importantly, Danny had the respect of the community he served. He could hunt down, chase, tussle with the best of them if they resisted, and then turn around and shake their hand when they got released from jail. It was not uncommon for an arrestee to thank Danny when the encounter was over. It was who he was.

Everyone loved him.

During the civil unrest in 2020, Danny changed. He was visibly tired. He began to self-isolate, and he lost his infectious smile. Throughout the month of July, I reached out to him (almost every day) because I sensed something was off. He stopped venting on social media, and I knew he was still struggling at home. Danny felt betrayed by the powers that be, both political and departmental leadership. He felt like a failure in the eyes of his colleagues because he could no longer support them. Moreover, he felt like the community turned on him. He questioned his overall purpose at home, at work, and in the community.

He felt betrayed in every aspect of his life.

I knew Danny was in trouble, but at that point, I didn't know what I didn't know. I did not know that his words and behaviors were specific clues. I did not know that his inner thoughts were darker than his outward expression. On July 27, 2020, a Sunday night, Danny and I texted back and forth the same way we did almost every day. I asked him if he wanted to meet up for a drink in the coming days, and without hesitation, he suggested a liquid lunch that Friday at Wildflowers, a local watering hole. He added that his son's birthday was the next day (Monday), and he was working Tuesday through Thursday. The conversation was brief. He did not seem interested in talking. It was inconsistent with our communication in recent days, but I did not think twice about it, at least not until Tuesday morning.

*Now it is **all** I think about.*

On July 29, 2020, the following Tuesday morning I woke up at five o'clock in the morning. It was expected to be hot that day, so I decided to get in an early bike ride. I went through my normal morning, pre-ride routine, leaving the house shortly after 6:00 a.m. I got out to the main road, heading west towards the river. Two-and-a-half miles in, at 6:22 a.m., my phone rang. It was my good buddy Sean, a detective from a neighboring department. He works odd, inconsistent hours and has a history of calling at unusual times. However, he would never call this early in the morning.

Something was wrong.

Again, I have a deal with all my friends. No matter what they did, no matter what happened, no matter what they needed, if they have an emergency, they can call me ***anytime***, and I will answer with the disclaimer that if I determine later that they woke me up or inconvenienced me because they were being drunk and stupid, they are subject to an ass whooping. So, true to my word, I answered the phone.

"Yo! Whassup, dude?"

"You good," Sean asked.

"Yeah, man," I replied. "I'm out for an early ride. What's up?"

There was silence.

Dead silence.

"I'm guessing you don't know," Sean said. "I assume no one has told you yet."

After a few seconds of silence, Sean asked, "You alone?"

"I'm on a fucking bicycle at six o'clock in the morning," I barked. "Yes! I'm alone. Just spill it; who is it and what happened?"

"Pull over and get off your bike," Sean politely directed.

This was not good.

"Where are you at," he continued.

I didn't know it, but Sean was already on his way to me. He knew that once he told me the "who" and the "what," I would no longer be able to respond to those simple questions. In my heart, I knew it then, too. That is why I followed his lead and did as he asked.

"It's Danny," Sean sighed. "He was found dead this morning in the trunk of his car in Plainsboro."

I was too shocked to reply.

"It looks like suicide."

I sat down next to my bike and started to cry hysterically. I experienced every emotion, from sadness to anger and betrayal—both Danny's and mine. Sean offered to pick me up, but I declined his generosity. I told him I was "fine" because that's what we do, even when we are far from it—*especially* when we are far from it.

I was able to collect myself for the ride home, but I don't remember it at all. I don't remember coming back to the house. The only thing I recall was my wife holding me on the couch. I remember being sad, but more so, I remember the feeling of guilt.

I should have known.

Shit, I knew it was coming because I asked him.

Point blank, I asked Danny if he was going to hurt himself. He told me, "No." There was so much guilt; maybe I asked the wrong question. He was honest with me. He said he was not going to hurt himself. In his mind, he may have thought that he was going to relieve himself of the pain. I should have asked the hard questions, "Are you suicidal? Are you planning to kill yourself?"

But I didn't.

I didn't know how to do that. I was just trying to be a good friend. I did not want to shame him or push him away.

I didn't know.

Danny's death changed me—instantly. I knew there was something I had to do, something to prevent other police officers from dying by suicide. I was determined to help those like Danny find the light at the end of the long, dark tunnel, the same tunnel I found myself in.

Wait a minute!

There I was, trying so hard to help everyone else, but I, too, was stuck in that same dark tunnel.

Was I next?

I wanted my pain to end, too.

I was in that same flat spin, heading out to sea.

Who was going to save me?

And how could I get someone to hear me and those like me? Since my retirement, I have been writing articles about policing and current events. I had 20 years of pent-up opinions that needed to be expressed. As an active-duty police officer, I was not allowed to engage in public discourse. Most departments have strict policy against it and for good reason. Police officers are supposed to remain neutral and without opinion. However, as humans, we most certainly have them. So, after I retired, I began to write and share all the thoughts I had been storing away all those years. Most pieces that I published were well received, and my many points were made, acknowledged, and even debated. Writing became therapeutic and quite cathartic. Paper has become a place where my thoughts can live outside of my head. It is a place where I can reflect on the all-consuming thoughts. On paper, my thoughts are separate from me, not clogging up and clouding my brain. When Danny died, I needed to write and express what was on my mind, not just for me, but for him, too. I needed to give Danny a voice, something he lost along the way. So, I sat at my computer later that night and 15 minutes later, I wrote this piece in honor of my friend:

When the roads of hurt, anger, and betrayal intersect, the streetlights can only shed so much light. No matter how hard we try to navigate through the darkness to find the right path forward, we can be blinded by our own emotion and go full throttle into a dead end. Here, we find ourselves at a point of no return, no matter how bright the light shines. Today, my friend came to this intersection and chose to hit the brick wall head on at the end of the road. He made this choice, knowing he was to leave behind what mattered most to him, his two young children. He made this choice, knowing the hurt they would endure. One can only imagine having to make that decision. What were the other factors that rose above living in a hurt locker, only to place your children in theirs?

As police officers, we face fear every day. We face horror our eyes can never unsee. We hear sounds that keep us up at night, and we endure tragedy that will take a lifetime to process. Yet, we press forward each and every day, living with the nightmares and the guilt. We drive onward to get to tomorrow because someone else will need us again. Where our road ends, is at the brick wall of betrayal and the subsequent distrust that follows. When it comes from our boss, we check out of work. When it comes from our partner, we kick them out of our car. When it comes from a friend, we delete them from our life. When it's our spouse, the burden can be too big to bear. We shield our kids and divert the focus. That diversion came by the way of suicide today, as my friend saw no path forward.

I will never understand why the daily calls, the texts of support, the plans we made just a few days prior, the next youth sporting event, the next vacation, the next whatever was not enough to light your path and overcome the darkness. So many cared so much, and still the only light you were able to turn toward was that of the Eternal.

Today, so many hearts are broken, as you have found your peace. I will never know the hurt you endured, the trust you lost or the love that failed you. I will never know how it is possible that the love of your children was not enough to get you through. May the demons that plagued you die with you. May those who loved you and cared for you find comfort in the memories they share of your laughter, sarcasm, good heart, and caring soul for others.

Police officers deal with the unthinkable, and in this culture war against the very individuals we depend on to protect us from evil, we have left them in the dark at an intersection of life that has no light at all. They have lost trust in the public, from whom they were betrayed. They have lost trust in their leadership, from whom they were betrayed. And now, they lose trust in loved ones, from whom they were betrayed. Just remember, my brothers and sisters, we will always have each other, from whom you will never be betrayed. Sadly, I believe there will be many more police officers unable to see the light through the darkness. However, I will always be there to answer the phone if you call. Just be strong enough to make the call. From there, I will take your hand, and we will walk together out of the darkness and into a place of light. Rest easy, Dan. May your memory always be a blessing. While I won't see you on Friday as planned, I will still share a beer with you, talking about you, instead of with you. I'll miss you, bro!

EOW 07/29/2020

I shared this article on my social media accounts, and it instantly caught the attention of many. From my brothers and sisters in Blue, elected officials, local media, and beyond. Unfortunately, it also got the attention of Danny's wife, and I'm sure his kids will read it someday. This was not something I thought about at the time I wrote it or even at the time I shared it. It was not until the funeral, when Dan's dad asked me to read it as a eulogy, that I realized its impact. That idea was quickly rejected and with good reason. I don't regret what I wrote, but I regret that it may have caused additional hurt to his loved ones.

Following the funeral, my article had been seen by more than 50,000 people. I hope at least one person who read the words also heard the message. If I was able to help even one person, it was worth it.

It would mean they heard me.

Someone who knew me reached out anonymously to a mutual friend, a man I will call Michael. Michael was a retired police officer from another town and the newly-minted county chief resiliency officer. He was the local go-to guy for cops who needed help in our county. He was a part of a new statewide program to bring a peer-to-peer support network (complete with resiliency tools) to law enforcement in New Jersey. This anonymous person reached out to Michael, expressing concern and asking that "someone reach out to Dave."

"Dave" being me.

This program was set up to help those still on the job. In law enforcement, with few exceptions, once you retire, you are outside of the social and communications loop.

You are all but forgotten.

After reading my article, that secret someone heard my cry for help and reached out on my behalf. Someone recognized the fact that just because a police officer retires, does not mean they should be ignored or forgotten. I am forever indebted to whomever it was that took the time to contact Michael, and I hope that someday that person will come forward, so I can thank them in person and tell them how much I love them.

I do love you.

Michael called me a few days after Danny's funeral. He asked me how I was doing. I am sure, by now, you know exactly what I said.

"I'm fine."

Michael did not accept my steel-plated response. He knew better. Unlike me in Danny's case, he knew how much I was hurting. He knew what questions to ask.

He knew what to do.

"Let's grab lunch tomorrow," he said, not giving me a chance to decline. Truth is, I don't think I could have declined. I saw Michael as my lifeline. I knew if I did not go to lunch with him, there was a great chance I would be the "next" statistic, leaving behind yet another widow and three more fatherless kids, not to mention confused family and friends. I would be another story that ended way too soon.

I was excited to meet with Michael the following day. He brought a friend along with him. I will call him Pastor Barry. Michael and Pastor Barry talked with me for hours, empowering me to move forward. I realized, I could either wallow in my problems and seek therapy, or I could be a part of the solution to help other cops, and at the same time, give myself the tools I needed to save my own life.

I chose option number two.

Michael told me that he would be hosting a Resiliency Program Officer (RPO) course at Pastor Barry's church. He invited me to take the class. I was one of the first retired officers in the county to become an RPO. I was also able to participate in the program, supporting retirees and active-duty members. Not only did the resiliency program save my life, but it changed it. I will forever be indebted to Michael for keeping me from becoming another statistic or the subject of someone else's article.

The Resiliency Program is founded in the teachings of Dr. Martin Seligman's "Applied Positive Psychology." The course is outlined in his book titled, *Flourish*, which I highly recommend. The program provides individuals with the tools they need to live life with purpose and a positive outlook. It also provides an avenue for the resiliency program officer to help others within their sphere of influence to do the same. In New Jersey, it provides a crisis safety net with the Cop2Cop hotline, dedicated to active and retired police officers and their families. They can call for help and follow-up care anytime of the day or night.

At the conclusion of the class, I had found a new mission and purpose. My life had new significance. As a police officer, my purpose was to help others. After I retired, I no longer had that same sense of purpose. When I became an RPO, I realized that helping others was still my reason for being, and it was time to help my own, my brothers and sisters in blue. I was still a part of the fraternity, only in a new role. I networked with local departments, the county prosecutor's office, and anyone in the law enforcement community I could think of. I had all these new tools, and I could not wait to use them.

I still reflect on that awful morning I was driving home from work, sitting at a traffic light with my gun in my lap, planning to end my life within the 90 seconds it would take me to park my car. I think back on the moment my son reached out to say good morning. I was distracted from completing my suicide. That was a very specific incident, a single moment in time.

Rock bottom.

My post-retirement depression was like death by a thousand cuts. Danny's suicide helped me realize that. In a way, it justified my own suicidal thoughts at the time. Michael was the second phone call that distracted me, the moment that saved me. It was the opportunity that gave me a newfound purpose.

Brother, this chapter is dedicated to you!

Michael, his wife, Dee, and the state's chief resilience officer formed the non-profit organization Resilient Minds on the Front Lines. I was trained by them to also facilitate the resiliency program and invited into this new family they created. It is there, along with the state program, that I continue to feed my passion and purpose, working to bring the "Pre-Boom" tools and skills for post-traumatic growth to officers and other folks across the nation.

CHAPTER TWENTY-THREE
Finding My Voice

I was never shot. I never had to shoot anyone, and I had no extraordinarily sexy, on-the-job adventure to share with others about my career that led me to believe there was power in my story. It was on my new quest to find ways to support my Blue Family that I realized there might be a way for my story to help others.

A while back, I crossed paths with military veterans who were providing transitional support to their fellow retired service members. In hopes of learning more, I sent out a few LinkedIn messages and connection requests. One of the individuals who responded was a retired Navy SEAL. We set up a call and spoke candidly about his work. He shared his story, explaining his unexpected separation from the Navy and how he found a way to survive both personally and professionally. He also explained how the stress is real when transitioning from any uniform service back into civilian life. His goal is to make the journey for others easier than his own.

Inspired by our conversation and anxious to bring such powerful support to the law enforcement community, I asked him if he would be willing to bring me into the fold and help me bring similar programs to transitioning cops. He responded with a chuckle and then paused.

Oh shit! Did I overstep?

I was still new at the whole networking thing. I did not understand business relationships yet.

Did I just slam a door shut?

I broke the silence with an apology. "Sorry, bro," I said. "Sorry if I moved forward too fast. I didn't mean to offend."

"No, man!" he replied, "All good. I am the one who should apologize."

I was surprised and confused.

The former Navy SEAL continued, "I have got to be honest. I don't get cops, and I don't think I can help your mission."

I was initially put off by his comment. I just assumed he was another cop hater, which surprised me because I thought if we were going to get support from anyone, it would be military folks.

The former SEAL added, "You guys are a special breed, and there is nothing I can do or say that could be taken with authenticity. You don't need to be engaged in a firefight every day to be a bad ass. Anyone with some basic training can do that. As SEALs, we train for specifically-planned missions until we get it right, and then we continue to train until we can't get it wrong. We make the rules of engagement and take control of the environment at all costs necessary. However, it takes a special kind of crazy to get up every day, leave your family, and deploy to your assigned area of patrol to face unknown circumstances. You fight by rules someone else makes up and who has never walked in your shoes. Your actions are required to be reactionary only and proactive action is sure to end your career and your freedom. You literally risk it all every day for the greater good, and then you are hung out to dry by your department and elected officials if your actions, right or wrong, make the news. I respect the shit out of all cops, but I can't relate. You guys are the real heroes of our society. You are the real bad asses of our generation."

Suddenly, I was silent.

Honestly, I did not know how to respond. I just had a storied United States Navy SEAL, one of our nation's most highly-qualified warriors tell me that cops were his heroes. It was a humbling experience, something I will take and reflect upon forever. That conversation also made me realize that my story was the same as 95 percent of all cops across the country. It was relatable to all of them. While the other five percent, those extraordinary stories of gunfights and one-of-a-kind heroics should be exalted. They are less relatable to most. I have put those folks on a pedestal, which always made me feel as though my career was, in some way, less significant. That is my problem, though … my hill to climb.

Trauma should not and cannot be a competitive sport.

After my new retired Navy SEAL friend told me he was not in a position to help me, he recommended I reach out to a woman named Sara. He explained that she had formed a group called "The Power of Our Story." It is a safe place for veterans and first responders to gather (virtually) and share their stories. It is also an opportunity to learn from and support one another as we transition back into civilian life—safely and together. We walk side-by-side, each finding our new purpose. The retired SEAL shared Sara's contact information with me, and I immediately reached out. I began an email exchange with Sara, and she invited me to join the group.

I'll never forget; it was a Thursday night. I logged onto the Zoom call. Sara and one other participant joined that night. It was just the three of us—me in New Jersey and the two of them in California. It almost felt like a set up, but I realized how lucky I was to have that one-on-one time with her. We spent over an hour getting to know each other. At the end of the call, I thought to myself, "This is a special woman with a special mission."

I looked forward to returning to meet more people and learn from their stories. I did, in fact, return the next week, the week after that, and in the years following, I have only missed two or three weeks—total.

Sara describes The Power of Our Story as, " ... *a community of protectors passionate about reducing stigma and providing a place of safety in a no-judgment zone for those needing a community to process the journey of mental and emotional adversities from the job. Through storytelling and conversation, we provide a personal and unique platform to support the transition process, share inspiration, and encourage that empowering spirit to get up and continue the fight. We are a tribe that grows stronger together. Our stories deliver HOPE.* "

My experience with this group is the very definition of resiliency. I came to it broken but because of all I have taken away (and returned in kind), I am okay now. In fact, I'm thriving, not just surviving. To present my comeback visually, this is how I see myself: br**OK**en. I have been empowered and inspired by the many stories I have heard from other members (regulars) and featured guests. I have also gained the courage and confidence to speak out loud and share my own story on multiple occasions.

When I was asked to share my 9/11 story, I had the courage to say yes. The virtual presentation was so well received that I was asked to present it at the Virginia Department of Criminal Justice Services' Impact on Trauma in Law Enforcement Conference one year later. I presented to a roomful, almost 200 people. I had the good fortune to share this experience with Michael and Dee, the founders of Resilient Minds on the Front Lines and who also presented at the conference. The same way that the Resiliency Program gave me tools, The Power of Our Story helped me reclaim my voice.

To this day, I continue to join the group almost every Thursday. I have gone from a fly on the wall to a storyteller, to a facilitator, to an interviewer, and to a host. I have grown in a way that I never thought possible. I have grown my confidence in telling my story on dozens of podcasts, in several periodicals, and now in this book. As much as all of this has helped me, I am not doing it for myself. I want to share my journey for my kids, my future grandchildren, and other police officers, first responders, and anyone who needs a little push to fight for tomorrow.

CHAPTER TWENTY-FOUR
Finding My Purpose

As a noun, the definition of the word *purpose* is the "reason for which something is done or created or for which something exists." As police officers, to which I am no exception, we enter the profession with a "purpose of serving others." We are a shared community, serving something bigger than ourselves. In terms of a verb, the definition of *purpose* is "to have as one's intention, objective or mission."

The language in the dictionary goes on to say, "purpose creates meaning, offers a sense of direction, and helps guide our paths, behavior, and goals when applied to our lives." When you consider the duration of our policing careers, we are fulfilling a mission within every shift. Upon retirement, however, we need to lean into the idea of charting a new path, creating new goals, and applying it to the next chapter of our lives. In other words, we need to redefine our sense of purpose.

For me, I used my background in drug enforcement and active-shooter response to build a consulting business that taught these valuable concepts to the civilian world. When developing this idea, I chased the money and not the passion. It was not until tragedy struck and my friend and Blue brother lost his fight for tomorrow, that I realized chasing money was not going to fulfill me. The work had no meaning.

It was not my purpose.

When Danny lost his fight, I knew it could have just as easily been me. I also knew he left behind an incomplete mission. Therefore, I promised I would pick up the fight for him and his kids … and for my kids. As parents, we would die for our children. As for me, I made a conscious choice to live for mine. I am going to live for my wife and for my family. I am going to live for my brothers and sisters in Blue. I am going to fight for all police officers and first responders who are frantically scouring that deep, dark cave, looking for the tools (the light, the love and the resilience) they need to climb out.

I found my purpose for existence, my PFE.

I am going to work every day for the rest of my life to stop cops from taking their own lives. I will do whatever I can to help them fight for one more day, but I need to help myself first. I need to put on my own oxygen mask before I help those to the left and to the right of me.

I was fortunate to have been given the chance to participate in New Jersey's Resilience Program. First, I was trained as a Resiliency Program Officer (RPO) by the state and then as a Master Resiliency Trainer (MRT) for Resilient Minds on the Front Lines. The resilience program gave me the tools I needed to repair what was broken inside of me. I was then given the opportunity to share those tools with others, teaching resiliency and consulting for the New Jersey Office of Resiliency for Law Enforcement. It is the first of its kind in the nation. I will never claim to be a master of the craft, but I will forever be a diligent student, continuing to share what I know and what I have experienced with others.

At about the same time I started my resiliency journey, I was introduced to Sara Correll and The Power of Our Story. It was in that safe space that I learned how important it is to listen to other people speak about their journey. In doing so, I quickly realized I was not alone in my challenges, and I was free to engage in the cathartic process of talking to others about the road I was on. I learned the art and the importance of vulnerability.

I spent my entire law enforcement career constructing an iron wall around me, protecting that which put me at risk of being emotionally exposed. Once I let that wall down, sharing myself in that safe space, I felt a sense of relief and freedom from all that haunted and imprisoned me over the last 30 years. I took control back by simply *choosing* to share.

It was in both my resiliency training and The Power of Our Story's platform that I found strength and courage. It was through this sense of empowerment that I learned how to love (really love!) for the first time. I can now give (and receive!) love with authenticity in a way that I never knew how before. That love brings me joy, a joy that I have not felt since the day I was sworn in as a police officer.

Law enforcement is much like owning a boat. You will enjoy it while you have it, but even the highlights are shadowed with a high level of operational stress. Your two greatest moments of ownership are the day you got it and the day you got rid of it.

Stay with me; I promise to bring it back full circle.

The transition from the job is also akin to the transition from boat ownership. Your friends stop calling. You have to find a new adrenaline rush. You have given up a part of your identity, and you are best served if you make the transition with purpose. Transitioning without purpose can lead to regret, and regret can lead to maladaptive decision making.

Writing checks you cannot cash, literally and figuratively.

They say the two best days of owning a boat are the day you buy it and the day you sell it. That is much like police work. Your two most exciting days, one's that *you* control, are the day you get sworn in and the day you retire. All the days in between, like boat ownership, are fun for sure, but require costly decisions and regular maintenance. If you fail to keep up, the price you pay in time will be much higher.

While some folks find purpose in doing what they know best and what excites them, I ultimately needed purpose to find myself. I sought purpose, but only saw what I perceived as purpose in the low hanging fruit. It was shallow and unfulfilling. It led down a path of least resistance, a path that continued to keep up the iron wall. When purpose finally found me, I freed myself from that which I feared most, my emotions.

Discovering that I could still connect with my fellow law enforcement officers and first responders, not just helping other people but helping my people, I found myself passionate again. That passion inspired me to do the hard work without the expectation of anything in return. It was simply that feeling of gratitude I got from positively impacting someone else's moment, day, week, year or life. To me, that is how I knew I found my purpose.

Gratitude

Gratitude is the foundation of my journey. Learning to give and receive it helps me recognize my purpose. According to the Oxford English Dictionary, Gratitude is defined as "the quality of being thankful, a readiness to show appreciation for, and to return kindness." Showing gratitude for the good that happens to you, helps you to recognize the good in your life. Accepting gratitude that others show you allows you to feel the good that you are doing for others. That give-and-take relationship is what fuels your purpose. Here are some easy ideas to express gratitude:

- **Start a Gratitude Journal**: It is as simple as buying a $0.99 notebook and writing down what you are grateful for each morning. Do the same thing at night before you go to sleep, noting even one thing for each entry reminds you of the positives in your life. This process motivates you to begin and end your day with a positive thought. After 30 days, this consistent practice rewires your neural pathways, and you automatically begin to experience more joy in your life. While joy and anger cannot exist in the same space, you find yourself smiling more and yelling less. You will experience more *happiness* and less *angst*.

I will compare gratitude to a purple truck. I am sure you just giggled to yourself, asking, "What are you talking about? I have never seen a purple truck." Well, now that we are talking about purple trucks, I guarantee you will see one on the roadway and then notice them more and more as time moves forward. The same goes for gratitude and purpose. Until you begin to think about it, you may not ever see it. However, when it is top of mind, you will see it everywhere.

- **Talk About Gratitude**: Discuss gratitude at the dinner table with your family. Ask each other what you are most grateful for each day. Use sticky notes to capture your thoughts and then put the notes on the wall in the kitchen. This will serve as a reminder every morning and every night of all that is good in your life. Try this exercise at work, too. It will change the office culture. It will encourage folks to be vulnerable yet anonymous, and others will become more compassionate as they see life from other people's perspective.

- **Create Gratitude Bags**: This is a simple gesture that costs little but makes a big impact on someone's day. My family hands out gratitude bags to ensure people feel noticed and appreciated. We fill small plastic bags with a few pieces of chocolate and/or candy and attach a handwritten note to it. We hand out these bags out to flight crews, gate staff, and TSA when we travel. We give them to hotel clerks and cleaning crews. We share them with lift attendants at the ski resort, gas station attendants, cab drivers, and service personnel, including first responders.

My favorite interaction was at Butternut Ski Mountain where, as a family, we spend most of our weekends in the winter. A young man was assigned to the men's bathroom in the lodge for eight hours. It was his job to keep the bathroom clean for guests. He continually had a mop in his hand or was washing the mirror, replacing paper products, or wiping the toilets and urinals after each use. While he was ever present and certainly working hard, he was hardly noticed by anyone using the facilities. One day, I gave him a gratitude bag, and his initial reaction was to throw it in the garbage, as if that was my intent for him as a patron. I quickly stopped him.

"That is for you," I said.

He seemed a bit confused, and so I explained.

"I wanted to thank you for all you do for those who visit the resort."

The young man was shocked and began to cry.

"No one has ever thanked me for doing my job," he said. "No one has ever acknowledged me at all."

"I know how that feels," I replied. "I see you and I appreciate you."

The joy on his face and in his heart was something I will never forget. A random act of kindness costs little to nothing, but it can change the world for someone else.

Random acts of kindness should not be so random. Be intentional and do good for others. Hold a door open. Pick up something that someone dropped. Let someone go before you in line. If the person in front of you seems flustered, genuinely tell them to take their time as you are not in a rush. Buy the coffee for the person behind you. Compliment someone. Say thank you. Kindness is a force multiplier. On the most basic level, doing something good for someone else without the expectation of getting anything in return, will not only make people feel good, but it will also make you feel good, too. Moreover, being kind to someone will likely inspire them to do the same for someone else, and before you know it, that kindness will come back to you, and you will be inspired to start the process all over again. Kindness brings joy to others, and as I mentioned earlier, joy and sadness cannot live in the same space. So, even in the darkest of moments, you can be the light.

For a while, finding my purpose was my purpose. Clearly, that is not sustainable, and I would need to support the journey with knowing the destination. However, one cannot underestimate the lessons learned along the way. The journey of finding my purpose helped me understand my "why." It was always there, but I never saw it.

From the stories of my ancestors to my childhood experiences, to my education and first responder career, it was always there. My "why" was always hungry, but it was easily fed by chasing after my dreams. For 20 years as a cop, it was fed the same diet, the same food, with the same routines and it was satiated. My "why" was disguised as my "who" and that clouded my purpose, especially during my retirement transition.

Once I recognized that my "why" was not tied to being a police officer, I was able to explore other acts that fulfilled me. I am driven by helping and supporting others to be the best versions of themselves. By doing so, I continue to give myself the chance to be the best version of myself. My fate is not to generate dollar bills through a career of building or selling widgets. I am not that creative to invent the next big thing or idea. I am not driven by tangibles, social status, or titles that some see as success. I am inspired by being part of someone else's significance, and to know that because of some value I was able to offer, that person is the best version of themselves and can do their part to make the world a better place for everyone else. That is what brings me joy and the feeling of having lived a purposeful life.

Furthermore, living a resilient life is not merely the art of bouncing back. It is the ability to bounce forward. It is about embracing the adversities in your life, being better today than you were yesterday, and setting goals and objectives to be even better tomorrow. Transgenerational trauma, adverse childhood experiences, lived experiences at home and at work are all waypoints along your journey that eventually lead to a fork in the road. They are the heavy bags you carry that represent the "who." That fork in the road is where you decide what to do with those bags and everything in them.

You can journey left, continuing to carry the load without purpose, having it weigh you down, wear you out, and burn a hole not only in the sole of your shoes, but far worse, in the soul of your being. Or you can choose to journey right, learning from what is in those bags, leaving behind the weight that no longer serves you, and marching forward with a defined purpose that serves your "why."

Mark Twain once said, "The two most important days in your life are the day you are born and the day you find out why." I do believe that when you find your why, you *will* find your way. We never have to forget about and burn down the house that built us, but if those four walls become your prison, recognize you have served your time and it may be best to move forward in your journey, build a new house, one that is filled with love, compassion, and empathy. Build a house where the mantle is created from wood of the old place, but where the kitchen table is new.

Auntie A. and Uncle Ant, that last line is inspired by you.

REFLECTIONS
Crystal Ball

To master the art of resiliency is to say you have reached a pinnacle and can go no further and learn no more. Your growth is maximized. This is contrary to the definition of the word "resiliency" and inconsistent with its principles. While I may be a master resiliency trainer, I will never actually master resiliency. However, I give you my word; I will forever be a student of the craft.

I see the world differently today than I did during my time as a police officer and during my transition into retirement from the job. I have learned to trust more, learn more, and love more. I am able to see past the evil and despair that fills the day of a law enforcement officer and find ways to recognize the good in people and surround myself with those who love me back. As humans, we tend to return to what is comfortable, even when that which feels comfortable is not what is good for us. I challenge you to get good and uncomfortable—live there. You will find it liberating, empowering, and inspirational. It only takes 30 consecutive days of engaging in an activity to convert it into a habit.

Take the risk!!

As I stare into my crystal ball and look towards tomorrow and beyond, it is fuzzy, like many of my past memories. I see pictures of winding roads that present no clear view of my destination. However, right in front of me, I can see the reflection of my gazing eyes, showing me exactly where I am right now. While I continue to dial into what comes next, I am learning to appreciate what I have right now and being where my feet are.

I am learning to value time, as it is the only constant. I am learning to embrace love, as that is what gives time its meaning. I am learning to love myself because that is what allows me to love others. I don't know what will become of me tomorrow or the next day, but I do know I will not let it define me the way I did when I was a police officer because I know *who* I am and that is something no one can ever take away.

I am a husband.

I am a father.

I am a patriot.

I am my brothers' and sisters' keeper.

I have found my why, and now I will find my way.

I am also honored and proud to share that I have been accepted into the University of Pennsylvania's Masters of Applied Positive Psychology (MAPP) program in the fall of 2023. MAPP is the world's first and most prominent degree program in this field, created by Dr. Seligman, himself. He is still a fundamental part of the program. As I study and work to become an expert in the field of positive psychology, I will leverage this opportunity to continue to give police officers and other first responders the tools to stay resilient.

I am grateful you have taken the time to travel along this path of my journey. You have traversed the chapters of my life through the written chapters in this book. I hope you have learned new things about yourself while learning some things about me. In the process, I hope you found inspiration to purposefully place a fork in the road you are on, a place where you can shed some of the weight from your past and create a new path for yourself. As you drive forward, don't forget to look into the mirror on occasion to see how far you have come.

I look forward to our two roads converging one day, an intersection where you and I can both pull over, bring value to each other's travels, and share our own personal road maps with each other. Until then, stay safe. Stay resilient and earn your badge every day!

With every sunset you experience, may you wake to a vibrant sunrise and clear blue skies that inspire the day ahead.
"Geh mit Gott. Ich liebe dich."
(Go with God. I love you.)

Bibliography

About Us. (2023). Retrieved from Citizens Behind the Badge: www.behindbadge.org

Adverse Childhood Experiences. (2023, February 17). Retrieved from Center for Disease Control: https://www.cdc.gov/violenceprevention/aces

Correll, S. (2023). *The Power of Our Story*. Retrieved from The Power of Our Story: www.thepowerofourstory.com

Kevin Hines. (2023). Retrieved from Kevin Hines Story: www.kevinhinesstory.com

Mercer County Resiliency Program . (n.d.). *Train-The-Trainer Student Workbook Version 11*.

National Law Enforcement Officers Memorial Fund. (2023). Retrieved from National Law Enforcement Officers Memorial Fund: www.nleomf.org

Officer Down Memorial Page. (2023). Retrieved from Officer Down Memorial Page: www.odmp.org

Police Unity Tour. (2023). Retrieved from Police Unity Tour: www.policeunitytour.com

Made in the USA
Middletown, DE
27 September 2023

39546461R00129